MznLnx

Missing Links Exam Preps

Exam Prep for

Retailing Management

Levy & Weitz, 5th Edition

The MznLnx Exam Prep is your link from the texbook and lecture to your exams.
The MznLnx Exam Preps are unauthorized and comprehensive reviews of your textbooks.

All material provided by MznLnx and Rico Publications (c) 2010
Textbook publishers and textbook authors do not particpate in or contribute to these reviews.

MznLnx

Rico Publications

Exam Prep for Retailing Management
5th Edition
Levy & Weitz

Publisher: Raymond Houge	*Product Manager:* Dave Mason
Assistant Editor: Michael Rouger	*Editorial Assitant:* Rachel Guzmanji
Text and Cover Designer: Lisa Buckner	*Pedagogy:* Debra Long
Marketing Manager: Sara Swagger	*Cover Image:* Jim Reed/Getty Images
Project Manager, Editorial Production: Jerry Emerson	*Text and Cover Printer:* City Printing, Inc.
Art Director: Vernon Lowerui	*Compositor:* Media Mix, Inc.

(c) 2010 Rico Publications

ALL RIGHTS RESERVED. No part of this work covered by the copyright may be reproduced or used in any form or by an means--graphic, electronic, or mechanical, including photocopying, recording, taping, Web distribution, information storage, and retrieval systems, or in any other manner--without the written permission of the publisher.

Printed in the United States
ISBN:

For more information about our products, contact us at:
Dave.Mason@RicoPublications.com

For permission to use material from this text or product, submit a request online to:
Dave.Mason@RicoPublications.com

Contents

CHAPTER 1
INTRODUCTION TO THE WORLD OF RETAILING   1

CHAPTER 2
TYPES OF RETAILERS   3

CHAPTER 3
MULTICHANNEL RETAILING-A VIEW INTO THE FUTURE   8

CHAPTER 4
CUSTOMER BUYING BEHAVIOR   11

CHAPTER 5
RETAIL MARKET SRATEGY   14

CHAPTER 6
FINANCIAL STRATEGY   23

CHAPTER 7
RETAIL LOCATIONS   30

CHAPTER 8
SITE SELECTION   31

CHAPTER 9
HUMAN RESOURCE MANAGEMENT   35

CHAPTER 10
INFORMATION SYSTEMS AND SUPPLY CHAIN MANAGEMENT   43

CHAPTER 11
CUSTOMER RELATIONSHIP MANAGEMENT   49

CHAPTER 12
PLANNING MERCHANDISE ASSORTMENTS   53

CHAPTER 13
BUYING SYSTEMS   59

CHAPTER 14
BUYING MERCHANDISE   61

CHAPTER 15
PRICING   68

CHAPTER 16
RETAIL COMMUNICATION MIX   75

CHAPTER 17
MANAGING THE STORE   79

CHAPTER 18
STORE LAYOUT, DESIGN, AND VISUAL MERCHANDISING   84

CHAPTER 19
CUSTOMER SERVICE   85

ANSWER KEY   87

TO THE STUDENT

COMPREHENSIVE

The *MznLnx* Exam Prep series is designed to help you pass your exams. Editors at MznLnx review your textbooks and then prepare these practice exams to help you master the textbook material. Unlike study guides, workbooks, and practice tests provided by the texbook publisher and textbook authors, *MznLnx* gives you **all** of the material in each chapter in exam form, not just samples, so you can be sure to nail your exam.

MECHANICAL

The MznLnx Exam Prep series creates exams that will help you learn the subject matter as well as test you on your understanding. Each question is designed to help you master the concept. Just working through the exams, you gain an understanding of the subject--its a simple mechanical process that produces success.

INTEGRATED STUDY GUIDE AND REVIEW

MznLnx is not just a set of exams designed to test you, its also a comprehensive review of the subject content. Each exam question is also a review of the concept, making sure that you will get the answer correct without having to go to other sources of material. You learn as you go! Its the easiest way to pass an exam.

HUMOR

Studying can be tedious and dry. MznLnx's instructional design includes moderate humor within the exam questions on occassion, to break the tedium and revitalize the brain

Chapter 1. INTRODUCTION TO THE WORLD OF RETAILING

1. _____ is one of the four elements of marketing mix. An organization or set of organizations (go-betweens) involved in the process of making a product or service available for use or consumption by a consumer or business user.

The other three parts of the marketing mix are product, pricing, and promotion.

   a. Job creation programs
   b. Matching theory
   c. Missing completely at random
   d. Distribution

2. _____ consists of the sale of goods or merchandise from a fixed location, such as a department store, boutique or kiosk in small or individual lots for direct consumption by the purchaser. _____ may include subordinated services, such as delivery. Purchasers may be individuals or businesses.
   a. Planogram
   b. 28-hour day
   c. Retailing
   d. 1990 Clean Air Act

3. _____ is a term defined by the Oxford English Dictionary as an individual's 'course or progress through life '. It is usually considered to pertain to remunerative work (and sometimes also formal education.)

The etymology of the term is somewhat ironic in that it comes from the Latin word carrera, which means race .

   a. Spatial mismatch
   b. Nursing shortage
   c. Career
   d. Career planning

4. A _____ is a list of the general tasks and responsibilities of a position. Typically, it also includes to whom the position reports, specifications such as the qualifications needed by the person in the job, salary range for the position, etc. A _____ is usually developed by conducting a job analysis, which includes examining the tasks and sequences of tasks necessary to perform the job.
   a. Recruitment advertising
   b. Job description
   c. Recruitment Process Insourcing
   d. Recruitment

5. In microeconomics and management, the term _____ describes a style of management control. Vertically integrated companies are united through a hierarchy with a common owner. Usually each member of the hierarchy produces a different product or (market-specific) service, and the products combine to satisfy a common need.
   a. Vertical integration
   b. 33 Strategies of War
   c. 28-hour day
   d. 1990 Clean Air Act

6. _____ is a contract between two parties, one being the employer and the other being the employee. An employee may be defined as: 'A person in the service of another under any contract of hire, express or implied, oral or written, where the employer has the power or right to control and direct the employee in the material details of how the work is to be performed.' Black's Law Dictionary page 471 (5th ed. 1979.)
   a. Employment
   b. Exit interview
   c. Employment rate
   d. Employment counsellor

7. A _____ is a process in which a potential employee is evaluated by an employer for prospective employment in their company, organization and was established in the late 16th century.

A _____ typically precedes the hiring decision, and is used to evaluate the candidate. The interview is usually preceded by the evaluation of submitted résumés from interested candidates, then selecting a small number of candidates for interviews.

   a. Supported employment
   b. Job interview
   c. Split shift
   d. Payrolling

Chapter 2. TYPES OF RETAILERS

1. _____ is a term defined by the Oxford English Dictionary as an individual's 'course or progress through life '. It is usually considered to pertain to remunerative work (and sometimes also formal education.)

The etymology of the term is somewhat ironic in that it comes from the Latin word carrera, which means race .

   a. Nursing shortage
   b. Career
   c. Spatial mismatch
   d. Career planning

2. The 'business case for _____', theorizes that in a global marketplace, a company that employs a diverse workforce (both men and women, people of many generations, people from ethnically and racially diverse backgrounds etc.) is better able to understand the demographics of the marketplace it serves and is thus better equipped to thrive in that marketplace than a company that has a more limited range of employee demographics.

An additional corollary suggests that a company that supports the _____ of its workforce can also improve employee satisfaction, productivity and retention.

   a. Diversity
   b. Kanban
   c. Trademark
   d. Virtual team

3. The term '_____' refers to the concept of collecting information and attempting to spot a pattern in the information. In some fields of study, the term '_____' has more formally-defined meanings.

In project management _____ is a mathematical technique that uses historical results to predict future outcome.

   a. Regression analysis
   b. Least squares
   c. Stepwise regression
   d. Trend analysis

4. _____ consists of the sale of goods or merchandise from a fixed location, such as a department store, boutique or kiosk in small or individual lots for direct consumption by the purchaser. _____ may include subordinated services, such as delivery. Purchasers may be individuals or businesses.

Chapter 2. TYPES OF RETAILERS

a. Planogram
b. 1990 Clean Air Act
c. Retailing
d. 28-hour day

5. _____ in its literal sense is the process of transformation of local or regional phenomena into global ones. It can be described as a process by which the people of the world are unified into a single society and function together.

This process is a combination of economic, technological, sociocultural and political forces.

a. Collaborative Planning, Forecasting and Replenishment
b. Globalization
c. Histogram
d. Cost Management

6. _____ is the provision of service to customers before, during and after a purchase.

According to Turban et al. (2002), '_____ is a series of activities designed to enhance the level of customer satisfaction - that is, the feeling that a product or service has met the customer expectation.'

Its importance varies by product, industry and customer; defective or broken merchandise can be exchanged, often only with a receipt and within a specified time frame.

a. 28-hour day
b. Service rate
c. 1990 Clean Air Act
d. Customer service

7. _____ is an advertisement in which a particular product specifically mentions a competitor by name for the express purpose of showing why the competitor is inferior to the product naming it.

This should not be confused with parody advertisements, where a fictional product is being advertised for the purpose of poking fun at the particular advertisement, nor should it be confused with the use of a coined brand name for the purpose of comparing the product without actually naming an actual competitor. ('Wikipedia tastes better and is less filling than the Encyclopedia Galactica.')

In the 1980s, during what has been referred to as the cola wars, soft-drink manufacturer Pepsi ran a series of advertisements where people, caught on hidden camera, in a blind taste test, chose Pepsi over rival Coca-Cola.

Chapter 2. TYPES OF RETAILERS

a. Comparative advertising
b. 1990 Clean Air Act
c. 33 Strategies of War
d. 28-hour day

8. _____ is one of the four Ps of the marketing mix. The other three aspects are product, promotion, and place. It is also a key variable in microeconomic price allocation theory.
   a. Penetration pricing
   b. Transfer pricing
   c. Price floor
   d. Pricing

9. A _____ is a commercial building for storage of goods. _____s are used by manufacturers, importers, exporters, wholesalers, transport businesses, customs, etc. They are usually large plain buildings in industrial areas of cities and towns.
   a. 28-hour day
   b. 1990 Clean Air Act
   c. 33 Strategies of War
   d. Warehouse

10. _____ is a term used in marketing and strategic management to describe a product, service, brand, or company that has such a distinct sustainable competitive advantage that competing firms find it almost impossible to operate profitably in that industry. The existence of a _____ will eliminate almost all market entities, whether real or virtual. Many existing firms will leave the industry, thereby increasing the industry's concentration ratio.
    a. 1990 Clean Air Act
    b. 28-hour day
    c. 33 Strategies of War
    d. Category killer

11. _____ is a retail channel for the distribution of goods and services. At a basic level it may be defined as marketing and selling products, direct to consumers away from a fixed retail location. Sales are typically made through party plan, one to one demonstrations, and other personal contact arrangements.
    a. 33 Strategies of War
    b. 1990 Clean Air Act
    c. 28-hour day
    d. Direct selling

Chapter 2. TYPES OF RETAILERS

12. _____ are long-format television commercials, typically five minutes or longer.. _____ are also known as paid programming (or teleshopping in Europe.) Originally, they were a phenomenon that started in the United States where they were typically shown overnight (usually 2:00 a.m. to 6:00 a.m.)

   a. A Stake in the Outcome
   b. A4e
   c. AAAI
   d. Infomercials

13. A _____ is a non-sustainable business model that involves the exchange of money primarily for enrolling other people into the scheme, often without any product or service being delivered.

   _____s are illegal in many countries, including the United States, the United Kingdom, France, Germany, Canada, Romania, Colombia, Malaysia, Poland, Norway, Bulgaria, Australia, New Zealand, Japan, Italy, Nepal, Philippines, South Africa Sri Lanka, Thailand, Iran, the People's Republic of China, Mexico, Portugal and The Netherlands. These types of schemes have existed for at least a century.

   a. 1990 Clean Air Act
   b. 28-hour day
   c. 33 Strategies of War
   d. Pyramid scheme

14. _____ is a form of communication that typically attempts to persuade potential customers to purchase or to consume more of a particular brand of product or service. 'While now central to the contemporary global economy and the reproduction of global production networks, it is only quite recently that _____ has been more than a marginal influence on patterns of sales and production. The formation of modern _____ was intimately bound up with the emergence of new forms of monopoly capitalism around the end of the 19th and beginning of the 20th century as one element in corporate strategies to create, organize and where possible control markets, especially for mass produced consumer goods.

   a. A Stake in the Outcome
   b. Advertising
   c. A4e
   d. AAAI

15. _____ is used in marketing to describe the inability to assess the value gained from engaging in an activity using any tangible evidence. It is often used to describe services where there isn't a tangible product that the customer can purchase, that can be seen, tasted or touched.

Other key characteristics of services include perishability, inseparability and variability.

Chapter 2. TYPES OF RETAILERS

a. A4e
b. Up-selling
c. A Stake in the Outcome
d. Intangibility

16. _____ is used in marketing to describe the way in which service capacity cannot be stored for sale in the future. It is a key concept of services marketing.

Other key characteristics of services include intangibility, inseparability and variability.

a. Perishability
b. 28-hour day
c. 1990 Clean Air Act
d. 33 Strategies of War

17. _____ is the state or fact of exclusive rights and control over property, which may be an object, land/real estate or intellectual property. An _____ right is also referred to as title. The concept of _____ has existed for thousands of years and in all cultures.

a. Emanation of the state
b. A4e
c. A Stake in the Outcome
d. Ownership

18. _____ refers to the methods of practicing and using another person's business philosophy. The franchisor grants the independent operator the right to distribute its products, techniques, and trademarks for a percentage of gross monthly sales and a royalty fee. Various tangibles and intangibles such as national or international advertising, training, and other support services are commonly made available by the franchisor.

a. Franchising
b. 28-hour day
c. ServiceMaster
d. 1990 Clean Air Act

Chapter 3. MULTICHANNEL RETAILING-A VIEW INTO THE FUTURE

1. _____ consists of the sale of goods or merchandise from a fixed location, such as a department store, boutique or kiosk in small or individual lots for direct consumption by the purchaser. _____ may include subordinated services, such as delivery. Purchasers may be individuals or businesses.
   a. Planogram
   b. 1990 Clean Air Act
   c. Retailing
   d. 28-hour day

2. _____ is a form of communication that typically attempts to persuade potential customers to purchase or to consume more of a particular brand of product or service. 'While now central to the contemporary global economy and the reproduction of global production networks, it is only quite recently that _____ has been more than a marginal influence on patterns of sales and production. The formation of modern _____ was intimately bound up with the emergence of new forms of monopoly capitalism around the end of the 19th and beginning of the 20th century as one element in corporate strategies to create, organize and where possible control markets, especially for mass produced consumer goods.
   a. AAAI
   b. A4e
   c. A Stake in the Outcome
   d. Advertising

3. _____ is a marketing strategy 'in which one firm tries to distinguish its product or service from competing products on the basis of attributes like design and workmanship' (McConnell-Brue, 2002, p. 437-438). The firm can also distinguish its product offering through quality of service, extensive distribution, customer focus, or any other sustainable competitive advantage other than price. It can be contrasted with price competition, which is where a company tries to distinguish its product or service from competing products on the basis of low price.
   a. Non-price competition
   b. 28-hour day
   c. 33 Strategies of War
   d. 1990 Clean Air Act

4. In economics, business, retail, and accounting, a _____ is the value of money that has been used up to produce something, and hence is not available for use anymore. In economics, a _____ is an alternative that is given up as a result of a decision. In business, the _____ may be one of acquisition, in which case the amount of money expended to acquire it is counted as _____.
   a. Cost allocation
   b. Cost overrun
   c. Fixed costs
   d. Cost

Chapter 3. MULTICHANNEL RETAILING-A VIEW INTO THE FUTURE

5. In economics, _____ is the removal of intermediaries in a supply chain: 'cutting out the middleman'. Instead of going through traditional distribution channels, which had some type of intermediate (such as a distributor, wholesaler, broker, or agent), companies may now deal with every customer directly, for example via the Internet. One important factor is a drop in the cost of servicing customers directly.
   a. 1990 Clean Air Act
   b. Disintermediation
   c. 28-hour day
   d. Virtual enterprise

6. A _____ is a name or trademark connected with a product or producer. _____s have become increasingly important components of culture and the economy, now being described as 'cultural accessories and personal philosophies'.

Some people distinguish the psychological aspect of a _____ from the experiential aspect.

   a. Brand loyalty
   b. Brand extension
   c. Brand awareness
   d. Brand

7. Some people distinguish the psychological aspect of a brand from the experiential aspect. The experiential aspect consists of the sum of all points of contact with the brand and is known as the brand experience. The psychological aspect, sometimes referred to as the _____, is a symbolic construct created within the minds of people and consists of all the information and expectations associated with a product or service.
   a. Brand awareness
   b. Brand image
   c. Brand management
   d. Channel conflict

8. _____ is one of the four Ps of the marketing mix. The other three aspects are product, promotion, and place. It is also a key variable in microeconomic price allocation theory.
   a. Transfer pricing
   b. Penetration pricing
   c. Price floor
   d. Pricing

Chapter 3. MULTICHANNEL RETAILING-A VIEW INTO THE FUTURE

9. _____ is an organization's process of defining its strategy and making decisions on allocating its resources to pursue this strategy, including its capital and people. Various business analysis techniques can be used in _____, including SWOT analysis (Strengths, Weaknesses, Opportunities, and Threats) and PEST analysis (Political, Economic, Social, and Technological analysis) or STEER analysis involving Socio-cultural, Technological, Economic, Ecological, and Regulatory factors and EPISTEL (Environment, Political, Informatic, Social, Technological, Economic and Legal)

_____ is the formal consideration of an organization's future course. All _____ deals with at least one of three key questions:

1. 'What do we do?'
2. 'For whom do we do it?'
3. 'How do we excel?'

In business _____, the third question is better phrased 'How can we beat or avoid competition?'. (Bradford and Duncan, page 1.)

a. 28-hour day
b. 1990 Clean Air Act
c. 33 Strategies of War
d. Strategic planning

Chapter 4. CUSTOMER BUYING BEHAVIOR

1. A _____ is a name or trademark connected with a product or producer. _____s have become increasingly important components of culture and the economy, now being described as 'cultural accessories and personal philosophies'.

Some people distinguish the psychological aspect of a _____ from the experiential aspect.

   a. Brand loyalty
   b. Brand extension
   c. Brand awareness
   d. Brand

2. _____, in marketing, consists of a consumer's commitment to repurchase or otherwise continue using the brand and can be demonstrated by repeated buying of a product or service or other positive behaviors such as word of mouth advocacy.

   _____ is more than simple repurchasing, however. Customers may repurchase a brand due to situational constraints, a lack of viable alternatives, or out of convenience.

   a. Brand image
   b. Brand awareness
   c. Brand extension
   d. Brand loyalty

3. _____ can be regarded as an outcome of mental processes (cognitive process) leading to the selection of a course of action among several alternatives. Every _____ process produces a final choice. The output can be an action or an opinion of choice.
   a. 1990 Clean Air Act
   b. Decision making
   c. 33 Strategies of War
   d. 28-hour day

4. _____ occurs when an individual's thoughts or actions are affected by other people. _____ takes many forms and can be seen in conformity, socialization, peer pressure, obedience, leadership, persuasion, sales, and marketing. Harvard psychologist, Herbert Kelman identified three broad varieties of _____.
   a. Role conflict
   b. Soft skill
   c. Social awareness
   d. Social influence

Chapter 4. CUSTOMER BUYING BEHAVIOR

5. A _____ is a group of people or organizations sharing one or more characteristics that cause them to have similar product and/or service needs. A true _____ meets all of the following criteria: it is distinct from other segments (different segments have different needs), it is homogeneous within the segment (exhibits common needs); it responds similarly to a market stimulus, and it can be reached by a market intervention. The term is also used when consumers with identical product and/or service needs are divided up into groups so they can be charged different amounts.
    a. SWOT analysis
    b. Customer relationship management
    c. Market segment
    d. Context analysis

6. In sociology, anthropology and cultural studies, a _____ is a group of people with a culture (whether distinct or hidden) which differentiates them from the larger culture to which they belong. If a particular _____ is characterized by a systematic opposition to the dominant culture, it may be described as a counterculture.

    As early as 1950, David Riesman distinguished between a majority, 'which passively accepted commercially provided styles and meanings, and a '_____' which actively sought a minority style ...

    a. 1990 Clean Air Act
    b. 33 Strategies of War
    c. Subculture
    d. 28-hour day

7. _____ is a form of communication that typically attempts to persuade potential customers to purchase or to consume more of a particular brand of product or service. 'While now central to the contemporary global economy and the reproduction of global production networks, it is only quite recently that _____ has been more than a marginal influence on patterns of sales and production. The formation of modern _____ was intimately bound up with the emergence of new forms of monopoly capitalism around the end of the 19th and beginning of the 20th century as one element in corporate strategies to create, organize and where possible control markets, especially for mass produced consumer goods.
    a. AAAI
    b. A4e
    c. A Stake in the Outcome
    d. Advertising

8. _____ is an integrated communications-based process through which individuals and communities discover that existing and newly-identified needs and wants may be satisfied by the products and services of others.

    _____ is defined by the American _____ Association as the activity, set of institutions, and processes for creating, communicating, delivering, and exchanging offerings that have value for customers, clients, partners, and society at large. The term developed from the original meaning which referred literally to going to market, as in shopping, or going to a market to buy or sell goods or services.

a. Marketing
b. Market development
c. Customer relationship management
d. Disruptive technology

9. _____ or _____ data refers to selected population characteristics as used in government, marketing or opinion research, or the _____ profiles used in such research. Note the distinction from the term 'demography' Commonly-used _____s include race, age, income, disabilities, mobility (in terms of travel time to work or number of vehicles available), educational attainment, home ownership, employment status, and even location.

a. Adam Smith
b. Affiliation
c. Abraham Harold Maslow
d. Demographic

10. The term '_____' refers to the concept of collecting information and attempting to spot a pattern in the information. In some fields of study, the term '_____' has more formally-defined meanings.

In project management _____ is a mathematical technique that uses historical results to predict future outcome.

a. Least squares
b. Trend analysis
c. Stepwise regression
d. Regression analysis

11. _____ is the process by which a new idea or new product is accepted by the market. The rate of _____ is the speed that the new idea spreads from one consumer to the next. Adoption is similar to _____ except that it deals with the psychological processes an individual goes through, rather than an aggregate market process.

a. Category management
b. Mass marketing
c. Diffusion
d. Value chain

Chapter 5. RETAIL MARKET SRATEGY

1. _____ consists of the sale of goods or merchandise from a fixed location, such as a department store, boutique or kiosk in small or individual lots for direct consumption by the purchaser. _____ may include subordinated services, such as delivery. Purchasers may be individuals or businesses.
   a. 1990 Clean Air Act
   b. Planogram
   c. Retailing
   d. 28-hour day

2. _____ consists of the processes a company uses to track and organize its contacts with its current and prospective customers. _____ software is used to support these processes; information about customers and customer interactions can be entered, stored and accessed by employees in different company departments. Typical _____ goals are to improve services provided to customers, and to use customer contact information for targeted marketing.
   a. Green marketing
   b. Marketing plan
   c. Customer relationship management
   d. Disruptive technology

3. A _____ is a process that can allow an organization to concentrate its limited resources on the greatest opportunities to increase sales and achieve a sustainable competitive advantage. A _____ should be centered around the key concept that customer satisfaction is the main goal.

   A _____ is a written plan which combines product development, promotion, distribution, and pricing approach, identifies the firm's marketing goals, and explains how they will be achieved within a stated timeframe.

   a. Marketing strategy
   b. Disruptive technology
   c. Category management
   d. Product bundling

4. Competitive advantage is, in very basic words, a position a firm occupies against its competitors.

   According to Michael Porter, the three methods for creating a _____ are through:

   1. Cost leadership - Cost advantage occurs when a firm delivers the same services as its competitors but at a lower cost;

   2.

Chapter 5. RETAIL MARKET SRATEGY

a. Theory Z
b. 1990 Clean Air Act
c. 28-hour day
d. Sustainable competitive advantage

5. _____ is, in very basic words, a position a firm occupies against its competitors.

According to Michael Porter, the three methods for creating a sustainable _____ are through:

1. Cost leadership

2. Differentiation

3. Focus (economics)

a. 28-hour day
b. Theory Z
c. 1990 Clean Air Act
d. Competitive advantage

6. The loyalty business model is a business model used in strategic management in which company resources are employed so as to increase the loyalty of customers and other stakeholders in the expectation that corporate objectives will be met or surpassed. A typical example of this type of model is: quality of product or service leads to customer satisfaction, which leads to _____, which leads to profitability.

Fredrick Reichheld (1996) expanded the loyalty business model beyond customers and employees.

a. 1990 Clean Air Act
b. 28-hour day
c. Customer loyalty
d. 33 Strategies of War

7. In marketing, _____ has come to mean the process by which marketers try to create an image or identity in the minds of their target market for its product, brand, or organization. It is the 'relative competitive comparison' their product occupies in a given market as perceived by the target market.

Re-_____ involves changing the identity of a product, relative to the identity of competing products, in the collective minds of the target market.

Chapter 5. RETAIL MARKET SRATEGY

a. Customer analytics
b. PEST analysis
c. Context analysis
d. Positioning

8. _____s are structured marketing efforts that reward, and therefore encourage, loyal buying behavior -- behavior which is potentially of benefit to the firm.

In marketing generally and in retailing more specifically, a loyalty card, rewards card, points card, advantage card, or club card is a plastic or paper card, visually similar to a credit card or debit card, that identifies the card holder as a member in a _____. Loyalty cards are a system of the loyalty business model.

a. 1990 Clean Air Act
b. 28-hour day
c. 33 Strategies of War
d. Loyalty program

9. A _____ is a commercial building for storage of goods. _____s are used by manufacturers, importers, exporters, wholesalers, transport businesses, customs, etc. They are usually large plain buildings in industrial areas of cities and towns.
a. Warehouse
b. 33 Strategies of War
c. 1990 Clean Air Act
d. 28-hour day

10. A _____ is a name or trademark connected with a product or producer. _____s have become increasingly important components of culture and the economy, now being described as 'cultural accessories and personal philosophies'.

Some people distinguish the psychological aspect of a _____ from the experiential aspect.

a. Brand loyalty
b. Brand awareness
c. Brand
d. Brand extension

Chapter 5. RETAIL MARKET SRATEGY

11. _____ is the strategic and coherent approach to the management of an organisation's most valued assets - the people working there who individually and collectively contribute to the achievement of the objectives of the business. The terms '_____' and 'human resources' (HR) have largely replaced the term 'personnel management' as a description of the processes involved in managing people in organizations. In simple sense, _____ means employing people, developing their resources, utilizing, maintaining and compensating their services in tune with the job and organizational requirement.

   a. Job knowledge
   b. Revolving door syndrome
   c. Progressive discipline
   d. Human resource management

12. _____ is the provision of service to customers before, during and after a purchase.

According to Turban et al. (2002), '_____ is a series of activities designed to enhance the level of customer satisfaction - that is, the feeling that a product or service has met the customer expectation.'

Its importance varies by product, industry and customer; defective or broken merchandise can be exchanged, often only with a receipt and within a specified time frame.

   a. 1990 Clean Air Act
   b. 28-hour day
   c. Service rate
   d. Customer service

13. _____ is an advertisement in which a particular product specifically mentions a competitor by name for the express purpose of showing why the competitor is inferior to the product naming it.

This should not be confused with parody advertisements, where a fictional product is being advertised for the purpose of poking fun at the particular advertisement, nor should it be confused with the use of a coined brand name for the purpose of comparing the product without actually naming an actual competitor. ('Wikipedia tastes better and is less filling than the Encyclopedia Galactica.')

In the 1980s, during what has been referred to as the cola wars, soft-drink manufacturer Pepsi ran a series of advertisements where people, caught on hidden camera, in a blind taste test, chose Pepsi over rival Coca-Cola.

   a. 1990 Clean Air Act
   b. 33 Strategies of War
   c. 28-hour day
   d. Comparative advertising

Chapter 5. RETAIL MARKET SRATEGY

14. _____ is 'the action or practice of selling among or between established clients, markets, traders, etc.' or 'that of selling an additional product or service to an existing customer'. In practice businesses define _____ in many different ways. Elements that might influence the definition might include: the size of the business, the industry sector it operates within and the financial motivations of those required to define the term. The objectives of _____ can be either to increase the income derived from the client or to protect the relationship with the client(s).
a. Business networking
b. Yield management
c. Gap analysis
d. Cross-selling

15. _____ is one of the four growth strategies of the Product-Market Growth Matrix defined by Ansoff. _____ occurs when a company enters/penetrates a market with current products. The best way to achieve this is by gaining competitors' customers (part of their market share.)
a. 33 Strategies of War
b. Market penetration
c. 1990 Clean Air Act
d. 28-hour day

16. In microeconomics and management, the term _____ describes a style of management control. Vertically integrated companies are united through a hierarchy with a common owner. Usually each member of the hierarchy produces a different product or (market-specific) service, and the products combine to satisfy a common need.
a. 1990 Clean Air Act
b. 33 Strategies of War
c. Vertical integration
d. 28-hour day

17. A _____ is an entity formed between two or more parties to undertake economic activity together. The parties agree to create a new entity by both contributing equity, and they then share in the revenues, expenses, and control of the enterprise. The venture can be for one specific project only, or a continuing business relationship such as the Fuji Xerox _____.
a. Patent
b. Civil Rights Act of 1991
c. Meritor Savings Bank v. Vinson
d. Joint venture

18. An _____ is a person who has possession of an enterprise and assumes significant accountability for the inherent risks and the outcome. It is an ambitious leader who combines land, labor, and capital to create and market new goods or services. The term is a loanword from French and was first defined by the Irish economist Richard Cantillon.

a. AAAI
b. Entrepreneur
c. A Stake in the Outcome
d. A4e

19. _____ refers to the methods of practicing and using another person's business philosophy. The franchisor grants the independent operator the right to distribute its products, techniques, and trademarks for a percentage of gross monthly sales and a royalty fee. Various tangibles and intangibles such as national or international advertising, training, and other support services are commonly made available by the franchisor.

a. Franchising
b. 28-hour day
c. ServiceMaster
d. 1990 Clean Air Act

20. A _____ is a brief written statement of the purpose of a company or organization. Ideally, a _____ guides the actions of the organization, spells out its overall goal, provides a sense of direction, and guides decision making for all levels of management.

_____s often contain the following:

- Purpose and aim of the organization
- The organization's primary stakeholders: clients, stockholders, etc.
- Responsibilities of the organization toward these stakeholders
- Products and services offered

In developing a _____:

- Encourage as much input as feasible from employees, volunteers, and other stakeholders
- Publicize it broadly

The _____ can be used to resolve differences between business stakeholders. Stakeholders include: employees including managers and executives, stockholders, board of directors, customers, suppliers, distributors, creditors, governments (local, state, federal, etc.), unions, competitors, NGO's, and the general public.

a. 28-hour day
b. 1990 Clean Air Act
c. 33 Strategies of War
d. Mission statement

Chapter 5. RETAIL MARKET SRATEGY

21. A _____ is a documented investigation of a Market that is used to inform a firm's planning activities particularly around decision of: inventory, purchase, work force expansion/contraction, facility expansion, purchases of capital equipment, promotional activities, and many other aspects of a company.

Not all managers are asked to conduct a _____, but all managers must make decisions using _____ data and understand how the data was derived. So all managers need a reasonable understanding of the tools most used for making sales forecasts and analyzing markets.

   a. 1990 Clean Air Act
   b. Marketing research
   c. Market analysis
   d. Marketing research process

22. The general definition of an _____ is an evaluation of a person, organization, system, process, project or product. _____s are performed to ascertain the validity and reliability of information; also to provide an assessment of a system's internal control. The goal of an _____ is to express an opinion on the person / organization/system (etc) in question, under evaluation based on work done on a test basis.
   a. Audit committee
   b. Audit
   c. A Stake in the Outcome
   d. Internal control

23. _____ is a concept related to the relative abilities of parties in a situation to exert influence over each other. If both parties are on an equal footing in a debate, then they will have equal _____, such as in a perfectly competitive market, or between an evenly matched monopoly and monopsony.

There are a number of fields where the concept of _____ has proven crucial to coherent analysis: game theory, labour economics, collective bargaining arrangements, diplomatic negotiations, settlement of litigation, the price of insurance, and any negotiation in general.

   a. Trade credit
   b. Buy-sell agreement
   c. 1990 Clean Air Act
   d. Bargaining power

24. In economics and especially in the theory of competition, _____ are obstacles in the path of a firm that make it difficult to enter a given market.

_____ are the source of a firm's pricing power - the ability of a firm to raise prices without losing all its customers.

Chapter 5. RETAIL MARKET SRATEGY

The term refers to hindrances that an individual may face while trying to gain entrance into a profession or trade.

a. 1990 Clean Air Act
b. 28-hour day
c. Barriers to entry
d. Predatory pricing

25. _____, in microeconomics, are the cost advantages that a business obtains due to expansion. They are factors that cause a producer's average cost per unit to fall as scale is increased. _____ is a long run concept and refers to reductions in unit cost as the size of a facility, or scale, increases.

a. A4e
b. A Stake in the Outcome
c. Economies of scope
d. Economies of scale

26. Network externalities resemble economies of scale, but they are not considered such because they are a function of the number of users of a good or service in an industry, not of the production efficiency within a business. _____ are only considered examples of network externalities if they are driven by demand side economies.

Formally, a production function f is defined to have:

- constant returns to scale if (for any constant a greater than or equal to 0)
- increasing returns to scale if (for any constant a greater than 1)
- decreasing returns to scale if (for any constant a greater than 1)

where K and L are factors of production, capital and labour, respectively.

As an example, the Cobb-Douglas functional form has constant returns to scale when the sum of the exponents adds up to one.

a. AAAI
b. A Stake in the Outcome
c. A4e
d. Economies of scale external to the firm

Chapter 5. RETAIL MARKET SRATEGY

27. An _____ is the negative aspects of human activity on the biophysical environment. Environmentalism, a social and environmental movement that started in the 1960s, focuses on addressing _____s through advocacy, education and activism.

Major current _____s are climate change, pollution and resource depletion.

   a. A Stake in the Outcome
   b. A4e
   c. AAAI
   d. Environmental issue

Chapter 6. FINANCIAL STRATEGY

1. _____, Gross profit margin or Gross Profit Rate can be defined as the amount of contribution to the business enterprise, after paying for direct-fixed and direct-variable unit costs, required to cover overheads (fixed commitments) and provide a buffer for unknown items. It expresses the relationship between gross profit and sales revenue.

It can be expressed in absolute terms:

Gross Profit = Revenue − Cost of Sales

or as the ratio of gross profit to sales revenue, usually in the form of a percentage:

_____ Percentage = (Revenue-Cost of Sales)/Revenue

Cost of Sales includes variable costs and fixed costs directly linked to the product, such as material and labor.

 a. Profit maximization
 b. 1990 Clean Air Act
 c. Profit margin
 d. Gross margin

2. In accounting, _____ or sales profit is the difference between revenue and the cost of making a product or providing a service, before deducting overhead, payroll, taxation, and interest payments. Note that this is different from operating profit (earnings before interest and taxes.)

Net sales are calculated:

    Net sales = Sales - Sales returns and allowances.

 a. Gross profit margin
 b. Capital budgeting
 c. Cash flow
 d. Gross profit

3. An _____, operating expenditure, operational expense, operational expenditure or OPEX is an on-going cost for running a product, business, or system. Its counterpart, a capital expenditure (CAPEX), is the cost of developing or providing non-consumable parts for the product or system. For example, the purchase of a photocopier is the CAPEX, and the annual paper and toner cost is the OPEX.
 a. A4e
 b. Operating expense
 c. A Stake in the Outcome
 d. AAAI

Chapter 6. FINANCIAL STRATEGY

4. _____ relates to the cost of borrowing money. It is the price that a lender charges a borrower for the use of the lender's money. _____ is different from OPEX and CAPEX, for it relates to the capital structure of a company.

   a. A4e
   b. A Stake in the Outcome
   c. AAAI
   d. Interest expense

5. In business and finance accounting, _____ is equal to the gross profit minus overheads minus interest payable plus/minus one off items for a given time period (usually: accounting period.)

   A common synonym for '_____' when discussing financial statements (which include a balance sheet and an income statement) is the bottom line. This term results from the traditional appearance of an income statement which shows all allocated revenues and expenses over a specified time period with the resulting summation on the bottom line of the report.

   a. Matching principle
   b. Treasury stock
   c. Generally accepted accounting principles
   d. Net profit

6. Profit margin, net margin, _____ or net profit ratio all refer to a measure of profitability. It is calculated by finding the net profit as a percentage of the revenue.

   The profit margin is mostly used for internal comparison.

   a. Profit maximization
   b. Profit margin
   c. 1990 Clean Air Act
   d. Net profit margin

7. _____, net margin, net _____ or net profit ratio all refer to a measure of profitability. It is calculated by finding the net profit as a percentage of the revenue.

$$\text{Net profit margin} = \frac{\text{Net profit (after taxes)}}{\text{Revenue}} \times 100\%$$

Chapter 6. FINANCIAL STRATEGY

The _____ is mostly used for internal comparison.

a. 1990 Clean Air Act
b. Profit maximization
c. Net profit margin
d. Profit margin

8. In business and accounting, _____s are everything of value that is owned by a person or company. Any property or object of value that one possesses, usually considered as applicable to the payment of one's debts is considered an _____. Simplistically stated, _____s are things of value that can be readily converted into cash.

a. A4e
b. A Stake in the Outcome
c. AAAI
d. Asset

9. In accounting, a _____ is an asset on the balance sheet which is expected to be sold or otherwise used up in the near future, usually within one year, or one business cycle - whichever is longer. Typical _____s include cash, cash equivalents, accounts receivable, inventory, the portion of prepaid accounts which will be used within a year, and short-term investments.

On the balance sheet, assets will typically be classified into _____s and long-term assets.

a. Current asset
b. Matching principle
c. Net income
d. Treasury stock

10. In a human resources context, _____ or labor _____ is the rate at which an employer gains and loses employees. Simple ways to describe it are 'how long employees tend to stay' or 'the rate of traffic through the revolving door.' _____ is measured for individual companies and for their industry as a whole. If an employer is said to have a high _____ relative to its competitors, it means that employees of that company have a shorter average tenure than those of other companies in the same industry.

a. Career portfolios
b. Ten year occupational employment projection
c. Continuous
d. Turnover

Chapter 6. FINANCIAL STRATEGY

11. _____ is one of a series of accounting transactions dealing with the billing of customers who owe money to a person, company or organization for goods and services that have been provided to the customer. In most business entities this is typically done by generating an invoice and mailing or electronically delivering it to the customer, who in turn must pay it within an established timeframe called credit or payment terms.

An example of a common payment term is Net 30, meaning payment is due in the amount of the invoice 30 days from the date of invoice.

    a. A Stake in the Outcome
    b. Other revenue
    c. Accumulated Depreciation
    d. Accounts receivable

12. The _____ is an equation that equals the cost of goods sold divided by the average inventory. Average inventory equals beginning inventory plus ending inventory divided by 2.

The formula for _____ :

[×]>

The formula for average inventory:

[×]>

A low turnover rate may point to overstocking, obsolescence, or deficiencies in the product line or marketing effort.

    a. A Stake in the Outcome
    b. A4e
    c. Inventory turnover
    d. Asset turnover

13. _____ plant, and equipment, is a term used in accountancy for assets and property which cannot easily be converted into cash. This can be compared with current assets such as cash or bank accounts, which are described as liquid assets. In most cases, only tangible assets are referred to as fixed.

Chapter 6. FINANCIAL STRATEGY

a. 1990 Clean Air Act
b. Fixed asset
c. 33 Strategies of War
d. 28-hour day

14. _____ is a financial ratio that measures the efficiency of a company's use of its assets in generating sales revenue or sales income to the company.

$$Asset\ Turnover = \frac{Sales}{Average\ Total\ Assets}$$

- 'Sales' is the value of 'Net Sales' or 'Sales' from the company's income statement
- 'Average Total Assets' is the value of 'Total assets' from the company's balance sheet in the beginning and the end of the fiscal period divided by 2.

a. Asset turnover
b. A4e
c. A Stake in the Outcome
d. Inventory turnover

15. _____ is a file or account that contains money that a person or company owes to suppliers, but has not paid yet (a form of debt.) When you receive an invoice you add it to the file, and then you remove it when you pay. Thus, the A/P is a form of credit that suppliers offer to their purchasers by allowing them to pay for a product or service after it has already been received.
    a. Other revenue
    b. Accounts payable
    c. A Stake in the Outcome
    d. Accounts receivable

16. In finance, _____ are considered liabilities of the business that are to be settled in cash within the fiscal year or the operating cycle, whichever period is longer.

For example accounts payable for goods, services or supplies that were purchased for use in the operation of the business and payable within a normal period of time would be _____.

Bonds, mortgages and loans that are payable over a term exceeding one year would be fixed liabilities.

Chapter 6. FINANCIAL STRATEGY

a. Current liabilities
b. Generally accepted accounting principles
c. Matching principle
d. Depreciation

17. _____ is a form of corporate equity ownership, a type of security. It is called 'common' to distinguish it from preferred stock. In the event of bankruptcy, _____ investors receive their funds after preferred stock holders, bondholders, creditors, etc.

a. 1990 Clean Air Act
b. Free riding
c. Common stock
d. Stockholder

18. The _____ percentage shows how profitable a company's assets are in generating revenue.

_____ can be computed as:

$$ROA = \frac{\text{Net Income} + \text{Interest Expense} - \text{Interest Tax savings}}{\text{Average Total Assets}}$$

This number tells you what the company can do with what it has, i.e. how many dollars of earnings they derive from each dollar of assets they control. Its a useful number for comparing competing companies in the same industry.

a. Return on assets
b. P/E ratio
c. Return on equity
d. Return on Capital Employed

19. _____ is a unique identifier for each distinct product and service that can be purchased. Usage of the _____ system is rooted in data management, enabling the merchant to systematically track their inventory, such as in warehouses and retail outlets, and are often assigned and serialized at the merchant level. Each _____ is attached to an item, variant, product line, bundle, service, fee, or attachment.

a. 28-hour day
b. Stock keeping unit
c. 1990 Clean Air Act
d. 33 Strategies of War

Chapter 6. FINANCIAL STRATEGY

20. _____ is a concept in ethics with several meanings. It is often used synonymously with such concepts as responsibility, answerability, enforcement, blameworthiness, liability and other terms associated with the expectation of account-giving. As an aspect of governance, it has been central to discussions related to problems in both the public and private (corporation) worlds.

a. A Stake in the Outcome
b. A4e
c. Usury
d. Accountability

21. _____ refers to metrics and measures of output from production processes, per unit of input. Labor _____, for example, is typically measured as a ratio of output per labor-hour, an input. _____ may be conceived of as a metrics of the technical or engineering efficiency of production.

a. Remanufacturing
b. Value engineering
c. Master production schedule
d. Productivity

Chapter 7. RETAIL LOCATIONS

1. _____ consists of the sale of goods or merchandise from a fixed location, such as a department store, boutique or kiosk in small or individual lots for direct consumption by the purchaser. _____ may include subordinated services, such as delivery. Purchasers may be individuals or businesses.
   a. Retailing
   b. Planogram
   c. 28-hour day
   d. 1990 Clean Air Act

2. _____ consists of the processes a company uses to track and organize its contacts with its current and prospective customers. _____ software is used to support these processes; information about customers and customer interactions can be entered, stored and accessed by employees in different company departments. Typical _____ goals are to improve services provided to customers, and to use customer contact information for targeted marketing.
   a. Green marketing
   b. Marketing plan
   c. Disruptive technology
   d. Customer relationship management

3. An _____ is the negative aspects of human activity on the biophysical environment. Environmentalism, a social and environmental movement that started in the 1960s, focuses on addressing _____s through advocacy, education and activism.

   Major current _____s are climate change, pollution and resource depletion.

   a. Environmental issue
   b. AAAI
   c. A Stake in the Outcome
   d. A4e

Chapter 8. SITE SELECTION

1. _____ consists of the sale of goods or merchandise from a fixed location, such as a department store, boutique or kiosk in small or individual lots for direct consumption by the purchaser. _____ may include subordinated services, such as delivery. Purchasers may be individuals or businesses.
   a. Planogram
   b. Retailing
   c. 28-hour day
   d. 1990 Clean Air Act

2. _____ consists of the processes a company uses to track and organize its contacts with its current and prospective customers. _____ software is used to support these processes; information about customers and customer interactions can be entered, stored and accessed by employees in different company departments. Typical _____ goals are to improve services provided to customers, and to use customer contact information for targeted marketing.
   a. Marketing plan
   b. Disruptive technology
   c. Green marketing
   d. Customer relationship management

3. _____, in microeconomics, are the cost advantages that a business obtains due to expansion. They are factors that cause a producer's average cost per unit to fall as scale is increased. _____ is a long run concept and refers to reductions in unit cost as the size of a facility, or scale, increases.
   a. A Stake in the Outcome
   b. A4e
   c. Economies of scope
   d. Economies of scale

4. Network externalities resemble economies of scale, but they are not considered such because they are a function of the number of users of a good or service in an industry, not of the production efficiency within a business. _____ are only considered examples of network externalities if they are driven by demand side economies.

Formally, a production function $f(K, L)$ is defined to have:

- constant returns to scale if (for any constant a greater than or equal to 0) $f(aK, aL) = a f(K, L)$
- increasing returns to scale if (for any constant a greater than 1) $f(aK, aL) > a f(K, L)$
- decreasing returns to scale if (for any constant a greater than 1) $f(aK, aL) < a f(K, L)$

where K and L are factors of production, capital and labour, respectively.

Chapter 8. SITE SELECTION

As an example, the Cobb-Douglas functional form has constant returns to scale when the sum of the exponents adds up to one.

a. AAAI
b. A4e
c. A Stake in the Outcome
d. Economies of scale external to the firm

5. Franchising refers to the methods of practicing and using another person's business philosophy. The _____ grants the independent operator the right to distribute its products, techniques, and trademarks for a percentage of gross monthly sales and a royalty fee. Various tangibles and intangibles such as national or international advertising, training, and other support services are commonly made available by the _____.

a. 28-hour day
b. Franchisor
c. 1990 Clean Air Act
d. ServiceMaster

6. _____ is one of the managerial functions like planning, organizing, staffing and directing. It is an important function because it helps to check the errors and to take the corrective action so that deviation from standards are minimized and stated goals of the organization are achieved in desired manner. According to modern concepts, _____ is a foreseeing action whereas earlier concept of _____ was used only when errors were detected. _____ in management means setting standards, measuring actual performance and taking corrective action.

a. Turnover
b. Schedule of reinforcement
c. Decision tree pruning
d. Control

7. In economics, _____ is the desire to own something and the ability to pay for it. The term _____ signifies the ability or the willingness to buy a particular commodity at a given point of time.

a. 28-hour day
b. 33 Strategies of War
c. Demand
d. 1990 Clean Air Act

Chapter 8. SITE SELECTION

8. _____ is an organization's process of defining its strategy and making decisions on allocating its resources to pursue this strategy, including its capital and people. Various business analysis techniques can be used in _____, including SWOT analysis (Strengths, Weaknesses, Opportunities, and Threats) and PEST analysis (Political, Economic, Social, and Technological analysis) or STEER analysis involving Socio-cultural, Technological, Economic, Ecological, and Regulatory factors and EPISTEL (Environment, Political, Informatic, Social, Technological, Economic and Legal)

_____ is the formal consideration of an organization's future course. All _____ deals with at least one of three key questions:

1. 'What do we do?'
2. 'For whom do we do it?'
3. 'How do we excel?'

In business _____, the third question is better phrased 'How can we beat or avoid competition?'. (Bradford and Duncan, page 1.)

 a. 28-hour day
 b. 1990 Clean Air Act
 c. 33 Strategies of War
 d. Strategic planning

9. _____ is a broad label that refers to any individuals or households that use goods and services generated within the economy. The concept of a _____ is used in different contexts, so that the usage and significance of the term may vary.

Typically when business people and economists talk of _____s they are talking about person as _____, an aggregated commodity item with little individuality other than that expressed in the buy/not-buy decision.

 a. 1990 Clean Air Act
 b. 33 Strategies of War
 c. Consumer
 d. 28-hour day

10. _____ or _____ data refers to selected population characteristics as used in government, marketing or opinion research, or the _____ profiles used in such research. Note the distinction from the term 'demography' Commonly-used _____s include race, age, income, disabilities, mobility (in terms of travel time to work or number of vehicles available), educational attainment, home ownership, employment status, and even location.

a. Demographic
b. Affiliation
c. Adam Smith
d. Abraham Harold Maslow

11. In statistics, _____ refers to techniques for the modeling and analysis of numerical data consisting of values of a dependent variable and of one or more independent variables The dependent variable in the regression equation is modeled as a function of the independent variables, corresponding parameters, and an error term. The error term is treated as a random variable and represents unexplained variation in the dependent variable.
    a. Stepwise regression
    b. Trend analysis
    c. Regression analysis
    d. Least squares

12. _____ is a type of decision tree technique. It was published in 1980 by Gordon V. Kass. It can be used for prediction (like regression analysis) or for detection of interaction between variables.
    a. 33 Strategies of War
    b. 28-hour day
    c. 1990 Clean Air Act
    d. CHAID

13. _____ of the learning curve effect and the closely related experience curve effect express the relationship between equations for experience and efficiency or between efficiency gains and investment in the effort. The experience of 'learning curves' was first observed by the 19th Century German psychologist Hermann Ebbinghaus according to the difficulty of memorizing varying numbers of verbal stimuli, and subsequent learning about the complex processes of learning are discussed in the

The rule used for representing the learning curve effect states that the more times a task has been performed, the less time will be required on each subsequent iteration.

   a. Spatial Decision Support Systems
   b. Distribution
   c. Point biserial correlation coefficient
   d. Models

Chapter 9. HUMAN RESOURCE MANAGEMENT

1. _____ is the strategic and coherent approach to the management of an organisation's most valued assets - the people working there who individually and collectively contribute to the achievement of the objectives of the business. The terms '_____' and 'human resources' (HR) have largely replaced the term 'personnel management' as a description of the processes involved in managing people in organizations. In simple sense, _____ means employing people, developing their resources, utilizing, maintaining and compensating their services in tune with the job and organizational requirement.
   a. Progressive discipline
   b. Job knowledge
   c. Revolving door syndrome
   d. Human resource management

2. _____ consists of the sale of goods or merchandise from a fixed location, such as a department store, boutique or kiosk in small or individual lots for direct consumption by the purchaser. _____ may include subordinated services, such as delivery. Purchasers may be individuals or businesses.
   a. Retailing
   b. 28-hour day
   c. Planogram
   d. 1990 Clean Air Act

3. _____ consists of the processes a company uses to track and organize its contacts with its current and prospective customers. _____ software is used to support these processes; information about customers and customer interactions can be entered, stored and accessed by employees in different company departments. Typical _____ goals are to improve services provided to customers, and to use customer contact information for targeted marketing.
   a. Disruptive technology
   b. Green marketing
   c. Marketing plan
   d. Customer relationship management

4. In a human resources context, _____ or labor _____ is the rate at which an employer gains and loses employees. Simple ways to describe it are 'how long employees tend to stay' or 'the rate of traffic through the revolving door.' _____ is measured for individual companies and for their industry as a whole. If an employer is said to have a high _____ relative to its competitors, it means that employees of that company have a shorter average tenure than those of other companies in the same industry.
   a. Career portfolios
   b. Turnover
   c. Continuous
   d. Ten year occupational employment projection

Chapter 9. HUMAN RESOURCE MANAGEMENT

5. _____ refers to metrics and measures of output from production processes, per unit of input. Labor _____, for example, is typically measured as a ratio of output per labor-hour, an input. _____ may be conceived of as a metrics of the technical or engineering efficiency of production.
   a. Remanufacturing
   b. Productivity
   c. Value engineering
   d. Master production schedule

6. _____ or _____ data refers to selected population characteristics as used in government, marketing or opinion research, or the _____ profiles used in such research. Note the distinction from the term 'demography' Commonly-used _____s include race, age, income, disabilities, mobility (in terms of travel time to work or number of vehicles available), educational attainment, home ownership, employment status, and even location.
   a. Affiliation
   b. Abraham Harold Maslow
   c. Adam Smith
   d. Demographic

7. _____ is an increasingly broadening term with which an organization, or other human system describes the combination of traditionally administrative personnel functions with acquisition and application of skills, knowledge and experience, Employee Relations and resource planning at various levels. The field draws upon concepts developed in Industrial/Organizational Psychology and System Theory. _____ has at least two related interpretations depending on context. The original usage derives from political economy and economics, where it was traditionally called labor, one of four factors of production although this perspective is changing as a function of new and ongoing research into more strategic approaches at national levels. This first usage is used more in terms of '_____ development', and can go beyond just organizations to the level of nations . The more traditional usage within corporations and businesses refers to the individuals within a firm or agency, and to the portion of the organization that deals with hiring, firing, training, and other personnel issues, typically referred to as `_____ management'.
   a. Progressive discipline
   b. Bradford Factor
   c. Human resources
   d. Human resource management

8. _____ is generally a team of individuals at the highest level of organizational management who have the day-to-day responsibilities of managing a corporation. There are most often higher levels of responsibility, such as a board of directors and those who own the company (shareholders), but they focus on managing the _____ instead of the day-to-day activities of the business.

They are sometimes referred to, within corporations, as top management, upper management, higher management, or simply seniors.

Chapter 9. HUMAN RESOURCE MANAGEMENT

a. Functional management
b. Crisis management
c. Management development
d. Senior management

9. A chief executive officer (_____) or chief executive is one of the highest-ranking corporate officer (executive) or administrator in charge of total management. An individual selected as President and _____ of a corporation, company, organization, or agency, reports to the board of directors. In internal communication and press releases, many companies capitalize the term and those of other high positions, even when they are not proper nouns.
   a. CEO
   b. Director of communications
   c. Portfolio manager
   d. Chief executive officer

10. A _____ or chief executive is one of the highest-ranking corporate officer (executive) or administrator in charge of total management. An individual selected as President and _____ of a corporation, company, organization, or agency, reports to the board of directors. In internal communication and press releases, many companies capitalize the term and those of other high positions, even when they are not proper nouns.
    a. Chief executive officer
    b. Chief brand officer
    c. Financial analyst
    d. Purchasing manager

11. A _____ or chief operations officer is a corporate officer responsible for managing the day-to-day activities of the corporation and for operations management (OM.) The _____ is one of the highest-ranking members of an organization's senior management, monitoring the daily operations of the company and reporting to the board of directors and the top executive officer, usually the chief executive officer (CEO.) The _____ is usually an executive or senior officer.
    a. Value based pricing
    b. Product innovation
    c. Chief operating officer
    d. Supervisory board

12. While _____ literally refers to a person responsible for the performance of duties involved in running an organization, the exact meaning of the role is variable, depending on the organization.

Chapter 9. HUMAN RESOURCE MANAGEMENT

While there is no clear line between executive or principal and inferior officers, principal officers are high-level officials in the executive branch of U.S. government such as department heads of independent agencies. In Humphrey's Executor v. United States, 295 U.S. 602 (1935), the Court distinguished between _____s and quasi-legislative or quasi-judicial officers by stating that the former serve at the pleasure of the President and may be removed at his discretion.

a. Easement
b. Executive officer
c. Unreported employment
d. Australian Fair Pay and Conditions Standard

13. _____ is the process by which the activities of an organisation, particularly those regarding decision-making, become concentrated within a particular location and/or group.

a. Corner office
b. Chief operating officer
c. Centralization
d. Product innovation

14. _____ is the process of dispersing decision-making governance closer to the people or citizen. It includes the dispersal of administration or governance in sectors or areas like engineering, management science, political science, political economy, sociology and economics. _____ is also possible in the dispersal of population and employment.

a. Frenemy
b. Business plan
c. Decentralization
d. Formula for Change

15. In economics and sociology, an _____ is any factor (financial or non-financial) that enables or motivates a particular course of action, or counts as a reason for preferring one choice to the alternatives. It is an expectation that encourages people to behave in a certain way. Since human beings are purposeful creatures, the study of _____ structures is central to the study of all economic activity (both in terms of individual decision-making and in terms of co-operation and competition within a larger institutional structure.)

a. AAAI
b. Incentive
c. A Stake in the Outcome
d. A4e

Chapter 9. HUMAN RESOURCE MANAGEMENT

16. _____ refers to increasing the spiritual, political, social or economic strength of individuals and communities. It often involves the empowered developing confidence in their own capacities.

The term Human _____ covers a vast landscape of meanings, interpretations, definitions and disciplines ranging from psychology and philosophy to the highly commercialized Self-Help industry and Motivational sciences.

  a. A Stake in the Outcome
  b. A4e
  c. AAAI
  d. Empowerment

17. The term '_____' refers to the concept of collecting information and attempting to spot a pattern in the information. In some fields of study, the term '_____' has more formally-defined meanings.

In project management _____ is a mathematical technique that uses historical results to predict future outcome.

  a. Regression analysis
  b. Stepwise regression
  c. Trend analysis
  d. Least squares

18. The 'business case for _____', theorizes that in a global marketplace, a company that employs a diverse workforce (both men and women, people of many generations, people from ethnically and racially diverse backgrounds etc.) is better able to understand the demographics of the marketplace it serves and is thus better equipped to thrive in that marketplace than a company that has a more limited range of employee demographics.

An additional corollary suggests that a company that supports the _____ of its workforce can also improve employee satisfaction, productivity and retention.

  a. Virtual team
  b. Kanban
  c. Trademark
  d. Diversity

Chapter 9. HUMAN RESOURCE MANAGEMENT

19. _____ is a variable work schedule, in contrast to traditional work arrangements requiring employees to work a standard 9am to 5pm day. Under _____, there is typically a core period of the day when employees are expected to be at work (for example, between 11 am and 3pm), while the rest of the working day is 'flexitime', in which employees can choose when they work, subject to achieving total daily, weekly or monthly hours in the region of what the employer expects, and subject to the necessary work being done.

A _____ policy allows staff to determine when they will work, while a flexplace policy allows staff to determine where they will work.

a. Flextime
b. Bennett Amendment
c. Fiduciary
d. Certificate of Incorporation

20. _____ is training for the purpose of increasing participants' cultural awareness, knowledge, and skills, which is based on the assumption that the training will benefit an organization by protecting against civil rights violations, increasing the inclusion of different identity groups, and promoting better teamwork.

_____ has been a controversial issue, due to moral considerations as well as questioned efficiency or even counterproductivity.

According to Michael Bird, many project managers may feel that they are treading new territory as they lead project teams made of individuals from different cultures, heterogeneous mixes, and differing demographics.

a. Role conflict
b. Diversity training
c. Self-disclosure
d. Soft skill

21. There are two types of _____ relationships: formal and informal. Informal relationships develop on their own between partners. Formal _____, on the other hand, refers to assigned relationships, often associated with organizational _____ programs designed to promote employee development or to assist at-risk children and youth.

a. Real Property Administrator
b. Fix it twice
c. Human resource management system
d. Mentoring

22. The term _____ was created by President Lyndon B. Johnson when he signed Executive Order 11246 on September 24, 1965, created to prohibit federal contractors from discriminating against employees on the basis of race, sex, creed, religion, color, or national origin. In more recent times, most employers have also added sexual orientation to the list of non-discrimination.

The Executive Order also required contractors to implement affirmative action plans to increase the participation of minorities and women in the workplace.

   a. A Stake in the Outcome
   b. AAAI
   c. A4e
   d. Equal employment opportunity

23. In economics, the term _____ refers to situations where the advancement of a qualified person within the hierarchy of an organization is stopped at a lower level because of some form of discrimination, most commonly sexism or racism, but since the term was coined, '_____' has also come to describe the limited advancement of the deaf, blind, disabled, aged and sexual minorities. It is an unofficial, invisible barrier that prevents women and minorities from advancing in businesses.

This situation is referred to as a 'ceiling' as there is a limitation blocking upward advancement, and 'glass' (transparent) because the limitation is not immediately apparent and is normally an unwritten and unofficial policy. This invisible barrier continues to exist, even though there are no explicit obstacles keeping minorities from acquiring advanced job positions - there are no advertisements that specifically say 'no minorities hired at this establishment', nor are there any formal orders that say 'minorities are not qualified' - but they do lie beneath the surface.

   a. 1990 Clean Air Act
   b. 33 Strategies of War
   c. Glass ceiling
   d. 28-hour day

24. _____ is a contract between two parties, one being the employer and the other being the employee. An employee may be defined as: 'A person in the service of another under any contract of hire, express or implied, oral or written, where the employer has the power or right to control and direct the employee in the material details of how the work is to be performed.' Black's Law Dictionary page 471 (5th ed. 1979.)

   a. Exit interview
   b. Employment rate
   c. Employment counsellor
   d. Employment

Chapter 9. HUMAN RESOURCE MANAGEMENT

25. _____ is unwelcome harassment of a sexual nature, or based upon the receiving party's sex or gender. In some contexts or circumstances, _____ may be illegal. It includes a range of behavior from seemingly mild transgressions and annoyances to actual sexual abuse or sexual assault.

   a. 1990 Clean Air Act
   b. Hypernorms
   c. 28-hour day
   d. Sexual harassment

26. An _____ is a private computer network that uses Internet technologies to securely share any part of an organization's information or operational systems with its employees. Sometimes the term refers only to the organization's internal website, but often it is a more extensive part of the organization's computer infrastructure and private websites are an important component and focal point of internal communication and collaboration.

   An _____ is built from the same concepts and technologies used for the Internet, such as client-server computing and the Internet Protocol Suite (TCP/IP.)

   a. Intranet
   b. A4e
   c. A Stake in the Outcome
   d. AAAI

Chapter 10. INFORMATION SYSTEMS AND SUPPLY CHAIN MANAGEMENT

1. _____ consists of the sale of goods or merchandise from a fixed location, such as a department store, boutique or kiosk in small or individual lots for direct consumption by the purchaser. _____ may include subordinated services, such as delivery. Purchasers may be individuals or businesses.
   a. Planogram
   b. Retailing
   c. 28-hour day
   d. 1990 Clean Air Act

2. _____ consists of the processes a company uses to track and organize its contacts with its current and prospective customers. _____ software is used to support these processes; information about customers and customer interactions can be entered, stored and accessed by employees in different company departments. Typical _____ goals are to improve services provided to customers, and to use customer contact information for targeted marketing.
   a. Customer relationship management
   b. Marketing plan
   c. Green marketing
   d. Disruptive technology

3. _____ is the management of the flow of goods, information and other resources, including energy and people, between the point of origin and the point of consumption in order to meet the requirements of consumers (frequently, and originally, military organizations.) _____ involves the integration of information, transportation, inventory, warehousing, material-handling, and packaging, and occasionally security. _____ is a channel of the supply chain which adds the value of time and place utility.
   a. Third-party logistics
   b. Logistics
   c. 28-hour day
   d. 1990 Clean Air Act

4. A _____ is the system of organizations, people, technology, activities, information and resources involved in moving a product or service from supplier to customer. _____ activities transform natural resources, raw materials and components into a finished product that is delivered to the end customer. In sophisticated _____ systems, used products may re-enter the _____ at any point where residual value is recyclable.
   a. Drop shipping
   b. Supply chain
   c. Packaging
   d. Wholesalers

Chapter 10. INFORMATION SYSTEMS AND SUPPLY CHAIN MANAGEMENT

5. _____ is the management of a network of interconnected businesses involved in the ultimate provision of product and service packages required by end customers (Harland, 1996.) _____ spans all movement and storage of raw materials, work-in-process inventory, and finished goods from point of origin to point of consumption (supply chain.)

The definition an American professional association put forward is that _____ encompasses the planning and management of all activities involved in sourcing, procurement, conversion, and logistics management activities.

   a. Freight forwarder
   b. Packaging
   c. Supply chain management
   d. Drop shipping

6. The _____ of an edge is $c_f(u, v) = c(u, v) - f(u, v)$. This defines a residual network denoted $G_f(V, E_f)$, giving the amount of available capacity. See that there can be an edge from u to v in the residual network, even though there is no edge from u to v in the original network.
   a. 1990 Clean Air Act
   b. 28-hour day
   c. Residual capacity
   d. 33 Strategies of War

7. A _____ is a commercial building for storage of goods. _____s are used by manufacturers, importers, exporters, wholesalers, transport businesses, customs, etc. They are usually large plain buildings in industrial areas of cities and towns.
   a. Warehouse
   b. 1990 Clean Air Act
   c. 33 Strategies of War
   d. 28-hour day

8. _____ refers to the structured transmission of data between organizations by electronic means. It is used to transfer electronic documents from one computer system to another (ie) from one trading partner to another trading partner. It is more than mere E-mail; for instance, organizations might replace bills of lading and even checks with appropriate _____ messages.
   a. A4e
   b. AAAI
   c. A Stake in the Outcome
   d. Electronic data interchange

Chapter 10. INFORMATION SYSTEMS AND SUPPLY CHAIN MANAGEMENT

9. An _____ is a private computer network that uses Internet technologies to securely share any part of an organization's information or operational systems with its employees. Sometimes the term refers only to the organization's internal website, but often it is a more extensive part of the organization's computer infrastructure and private websites are an important component and focal point of internal communication and collaboration.

An _____ is built from the same concepts and technologies used for the Internet, such as client-server computing and the Internet Protocol Suite (TCP/IP.)

   a. A4e
   b. A Stake in the Outcome
   c. AAAI
   d. Intranet

10. _____ is a concept that aims to enhance supply chain integration by supporting and assisting joint practices. _____ seeks cooperative management of inventory through joint visibility and replenishment of products throughout the supply chain. Information shared between suppliers and retailers aids in planning and satisfying customer demands through a supportive system of shared information.
   a. Timesheets
   b. Career portfolios
   c. Collaborative Planning, Forecasting and Replenishment
   d. Groups decision making

11. _____ is a recursive process where two or more people or organizations work together in an intersection of common goals -- for example, an intellectual endeavor that is creative in nature--by sharing knowledge, learning and building consensus. _____ does not require leadership and can sometimes bring better results through decentralization and egalitarianism. In particular, teams that work collaboratively can obtain greater resources, recognition and reward when facing competition for finite resources. _____ is also present in opposing goals exhibiting the notion of adversarial _____, though this is not a common case for using the term.
   a. 28-hour day
   b. Collectivism
   c. Collaboration
   d. 1990 Clean Air Act

12. An _____ is a private network that uses Internet protocols, network connectivity, and possibly the public telecommunication system to securely share part of an organization's information or operations with suppliers, vendors, partners, customers or other businesses. An _____ can be viewed as part of a company's intranet that is extended to users outside the company (e.g.: normally over the Internet.) It has also been described as a 'state of mind' in which the Internet is perceived as a way to do business with a preapproved set of other companies business-to-business (B2B), in isolation from all other Internet users.

Chapter 10. INFORMATION SYSTEMS AND SUPPLY CHAIN MANAGEMENT

a. A4e
b. A Stake in the Outcome
c. AAAI
d. Extranet

13. _____ is a form of communication that typically attempts to persuade potential customers to purchase or to consume more of a particular brand of product or service. 'While now central to the contemporary global economy and the reproduction of global production networks, it is only quite recently that _____ has been more than a marginal influence on patterns of sales and production. The formation of modern _____ was intimately bound up with the emergence of new forms of monopoly capitalism around the end of the 19th and beginning of the 20th century as one element in corporate strategies to create, organize and where possible control markets, especially for mass produced consumer goods.

a. A Stake in the Outcome
b. A4e
c. AAAI
d. Advertising

14. A _____ is typically described as a deliberate plan of action to guide decisions and achieve rational outcome(s.) However, the term may also be used to denote what is actually done, even though it is unplanned.

The term may apply to government, private sector organizations and groups, and individuals.

a. 33 Strategies of War
b. Policy
c. 28-hour day
d. 1990 Clean Air Act

15. _____ is one of the four elements of marketing mix. An organization or set of organizations (go-betweens) involved in the process of making a product or service available for use or consumption by a consumer or business user.

The other three parts of the marketing mix are product, pricing, and promotion.

a. Matching theory
b. Distribution
c. Job creation programs
d. Missing completely at random

Chapter 10. INFORMATION SYSTEMS AND SUPPLY CHAIN MANAGEMENT

16. A _____ for a set of products is a warehouse or other specialized building, often with refrigeration or air conditioning, which is stocked with products (goods) to be re-distributed to retailers, wholesalers or directly to consumers. A _____ is a principle part, the 'order processing' element, of the entire 'order fulfillment' process. _____s are usually thought of as being 'demand driven'.
   a. 28-hour day
   b. Distribution center
   c. Third-party logistics
   d. 1990 Clean Air Act

17. _____ stands for all operations related to the reuse of products and materials. It is 'the process of planning, implementing, and controlling the efficient, cost effective flow of raw materials, in-process inventory, finished goods and related information from the point of consumption to the point of origin for the purpose of recapturing value or proper disposal. More precisely, _____ is the process of moving goods from their typical final destination for the purpose of capturing value, or proper disposal.
   a. 28-hour day
   b. 1990 Clean Air Act
   c. Reverse logistics
   d. 33 Strategies of War

18. _____ is subcontracting a process, such as product design or manufacturing, to a third-party company. The decision to outsource is often made in the interest of lowering cost or making better use of time and energy costs, redirecting or conserving energy directed at the competencies of a particular business, or to make more efficient use of land, labor, capital, (information) technology and resources. _____ became part of the business lexicon during the 1980s.
   a. Outsourcing
   b. Opinion leadership
   c. Operant conditioning
   d. Unemployment insurance

19. A _____ is the period of time between the initiation of any process of production and the completion of that process. Thus the _____ for ordering a new car from a manufacturer may be anywhere from 2 weeks to 6 months. In industry, _____ reduction is an important part of lean manufacturing.
   a. Lead time
   b. 1990 Clean Air Act
   c. 33 Strategies of War
   d. 28-hour day

Chapter 10. INFORMATION SYSTEMS AND SUPPLY CHAIN MANAGEMENT

20. A _____ is a third party logistics provider. As a third party (or non asset based) provider a forwarder dispatches shipments via asset-based carriers and books or otherwise arranges space for those shipments. Carrier types include waterborne vessels, airplanes, trucks or railroads.

a. Drop shipping
b. Supply chain
c. Supply chain management
d. Freight forwarder

21. _____ is an advertisement in which a particular product specifically mentions a competitor by name for the express purpose of showing why the competitor is inferior to the product naming it.

This should not be confused with parody advertisements, where a fictional product is being advertised for the purpose of poking fun at the particular advertisement, nor should it be confused with the use of a coined brand name for the purpose of comparing the product without actually naming an actual competitor. ('Wikipedia tastes better and is less filling than the Encyclopedia Galactica.')

In the 1980s, during what has been referred to as the cola wars, soft-drink manufacturer Pepsi ran a series of advertisements where people, caught on hidden camera, in a blind taste test, chose Pepsi over rival Coca-Cola.

a. 33 Strategies of War
b. 28-hour day
c. 1990 Clean Air Act
d. Comparative advertising

Chapter 11. CUSTOMER RELATIONSHIP MANAGEMENT

1. _____ consists of the processes a company uses to track and organize its contacts with its current and prospective customers. _____ software is used to support these processes; information about customers and customer interactions can be entered, stored and accessed by employees in different company departments. Typical _____ goals are to improve services provided to customers, and to use customer contact information for targeted marketing.
   a. Marketing plan
   b. Disruptive technology
   c. Green marketing
   d. Customer relationship management

2. _____ consists of the sale of goods or merchandise from a fixed location, such as a department store, boutique or kiosk in small or individual lots for direct consumption by the purchaser. _____ may include subordinated services, such as delivery. Purchasers may be individuals or businesses.
   a. Retailing
   b. 28-hour day
   c. Planogram
   d. 1990 Clean Air Act

3. The loyalty business model is a business model used in strategic management in which company resources are employed so as to increase the loyalty of customers and other stakeholders in the expectation that corporate objectives will be met or surpassed. A typical example of this type of model is: quality of product or service leads to customer satisfaction, which leads to _____, which leads to profitability.

   Fredrick Reichheld (1996) expanded the loyalty business model beyond customers and employees.

   a. 28-hour day
   b. 33 Strategies of War
   c. 1990 Clean Air Act
   d. Customer loyalty

4. A _____ is a commercial building for storage of goods. _____s are used by manufacturers, importers, exporters, wholesalers, transport businesses, customs, etc. They are usually large plain buildings in industrial areas of cities and towns.
   a. 33 Strategies of War
   b. 28-hour day
   c. 1990 Clean Air Act
   d. Warehouse

Chapter 11. CUSTOMER RELATIONSHIP MANAGEMENT

5. _____s are structured marketing efforts that reward, and therefore encourage, loyal buying behavior -- behavior which is potentially of benefit to the firm.

In marketing generally and in retailing more specifically, a loyalty card, rewards card, points card, advantage card, or club card is a plastic or paper card, visually similar to a credit card or debit card, that identifies the card holder as a member in a _____. Loyalty cards are a system of the loyalty business model.

a. 28-hour day
b. 33 Strategies of War
c. 1990 Clean Air Act
d. Loyalty program

6. _____ is the process of extracting hidden patterns from data. As more data is gathered, with the amount of data doubling every three years, _____ is becoming an increasingly important tool to transform this data into information. It is commonly used in a wide range of profiling practices, such as marketing, surveillance, fraud detection and scientific discovery.

a. Data mining
b. 1990 Clean Air Act
c. Decision tree learning
d. 28-hour day

7. A _____ is a group of people or organizations sharing one or more characteristics that cause them to have similar product and/or service needs. A true _____ meets all of the following criteria: it is distinct from other segments (different segments have different needs), it is homogeneous within the segment (exhibits common needs); it responds similarly to a market stimulus, and it can be reached by a market intervention. The term is also used when consumers with identical product and/or service needs are divided up into groups so they can be charged different amounts.

a. SWOT analysis
b. Customer relationship management
c. Context analysis
d. Market segment

8. _____ is the activity that the selling organization undertakes to reduce customer account defections. The success of this activity is when the customer account places an additional order before a 12-month period has expired. Note that ideally these orders will need to contribute similar financial amounts to the previous 12 months.

a. Foreign ownership
b. Customer retention
c. Process automation
d. Business rule

Chapter 11. CUSTOMER RELATIONSHIP MANAGEMENT

9. _____ is the provision of service to customers before, during and after a purchase.

According to Turban et al. (2002), '_____ is a series of activities designed to enhance the level of customer satisfaction - that is, the feeling that a product or service has met the customer expectation.'

Its importance varies by product, industry and customer; defective or broken merchandise can be exchanged, often only with a receipt and within a specified time frame.

   a. Service rate
   b. 1990 Clean Air Act
   c. 28-hour day
   d. Customer service

10. _____ is an advertisement in which a particular product specifically mentions a competitor by name for the express purpose of showing why the competitor is inferior to the product naming it.

This should not be confused with parody advertisements, where a fictional product is being advertised for the purpose of poking fun at the particular advertisement, nor should it be confused with the use of a coined brand name for the purpose of comparing the product without actually naming an actual competitor. ('Wikipedia tastes better and is less filling than the Encyclopedia Galactica.')

In the 1980s, during what has been referred to as the cola wars, soft-drink manufacturer Pepsi ran a series of advertisements where people, caught on hidden camera, in a blind taste test, chose Pepsi over rival Coca-Cola.

   a. 1990 Clean Air Act
   b. Comparative advertising
   c. 33 Strategies of War
   d. 28-hour day

11. _____ is a form of communication that typically attempts to persuade potential customers to purchase or to consume more of a particular brand of product or service. 'While now central to the contemporary global economy and the reproduction of global production networks, it is only quite recently that _____ has been more than a marginal influence on patterns of sales and production. The formation of modern _____ was intimately bound up with the emergence of new forms of monopoly capitalism around the end of the 19th and beginning of the 20th century as one element in corporate strategies to create, organize and where possible control markets, especially for mass produced consumer goods.

   a. A Stake in the Outcome
   b. AAAI
   c. A4e
   d. Advertising

Chapter 11. CUSTOMER RELATIONSHIP MANAGEMENT

12. _____ is an integrated communications-based process through which individuals and communities discover that existing and newly-identified needs and wants may be satisfied by the products and services of others.

_____ is defined by the American _____ Association as the activity, set of institutions, and processes for creating, communicating, delivering, and exchanging offerings that have value for customers, clients, partners, and society at large. The term developed from the original meaning which referred literally to going to market, as in shopping, or going to a market to buy or sell goods or services.

   a. Customer relationship management
   b. Market development
   c. Disruptive technology
   d. Marketing

13. _____ is 'the action or practice of selling among or between established clients, markets, traders, etc.' or 'that of selling an additional product or service to an existing customer'. In practice businesses define _____ in many different ways. Elements that might influence the definition might include: the size of the business, the industry sector it operates within and the financial motivations of those required to define the term. The objectives of _____ can be either to increase the income derived from the client or to protect the relationship with the client(s).

   a. Yield management
   b. Gap analysis
   c. Cross-selling
   d. Business networking

Chapter 12. PLANNING MERCHANDISE ASSORTMENTS

1. _____ is a retailing concept in which the total range of products sold by a retailer is broken down into discrete groups of similar or related products; these groups are known as product categories. Examples of grocery categories may be: tinned fish, washing detergent, toothpastes, etc. Each category is then run like a 'mini business' (Business Unit) in its own right, with its own set of turnover and/or profitability targets and strategies. An important facet of _____ is the shift in relationship between retailer and supplier : instead of the traditional adversarial relationship, the relationship moves to one of collaboration, exchange of information and data and joint business building. The focus of all negotiations is centered around the effects of the turnover of the total category, not just the sales on the individual products therein.
   a. Product line
   b. Mass marketing
   c. Category management
   d. Customer insight

2. _____ is a ratio in microeconomics that describes a seller's income on every dollar spent on inventory. It is one way to determine how valuable the seller's inventory is, and describes the relationship between total sales, total profit from total sales, and the amount of resources invested in the inventory sold. A seller will aim for a high _____.
   a. Reorder point
   b. Finished goods
   c. 1990 Clean Air Act
   d. Gross Margin Return on Inventory Investment

3. _____, Gross profit margin or Gross Profit Rate can be defined as the amount of contribution to the business enterprise, after paying for direct-fixed and direct-variable unit costs, required to cover overheads (fixed commitments) and provide a buffer for unknown items. It expresses the relationship between gross profit and sales revenue.

It can be expressed in absolute terms:

Gross Profit = Revenue − Cost of Sales

or as the ratio of gross profit to sales revenue, usually in the form of a percentage:

_____ Percentage = (Revenue-Cost of Sales)/Revenue

Cost of Sales includes variable costs and fixed costs directly linked to the product, such as material and labor.

   a. Profit maximization
   b. Profit margin
   c. 1990 Clean Air Act
   d. Gross margin

4. The _____ is an equation that equals the cost of goods sold divided by the average inventory. Average inventory equals beginning inventory plus ending inventory divided by 2.

Chapter 12. PLANNING MERCHANDISE ASSORTMENTS

The formula for _____:

$$\boxed{}$$

The formula for average inventory:

$$\boxed{}$$

A low turnover rate may point to overstocking, obsolescence, or deficiencies in the product line or marketing effort.

a. A4e
b. Inventory turnover
c. Asset turnover
d. A Stake in the Outcome

5. In a human resources context, _____ or labor _____ is the rate at which an employer gains and loses employees. Simple ways to describe it are 'how long employees tend to stay' or 'the rate of traffic through the revolving door.' _____ is measured for individual companies and for their industry as a whole. If an employer is said to have a high _____ relative to its competitors, it means that employees of that company have a shorter average tenure than those of other companies in the same industry.

a. Ten year occupational employment projection
b. Career portfolios
c. Continuous
d. Turnover

6. _____ is the process of estimation in unknown situations. Prediction is a similar, but more general term. Both can refer to estimation of time series, cross-sectional or longitudinal data.

a. 33 Strategies of War
b. Forecasting
c. 1990 Clean Air Act
d. 28-hour day

7. The term '_____' refers to the concept of collecting information and attempting to spot a pattern in the information. In some fields of study, the term '_____' has more formally-defined meanings.

Chapter 12. PLANNING MERCHANDISE ASSORTMENTS

In project management _____ is a mathematical technique that uses historical results to predict future outcome.

a. Stepwise regression
b. Regression analysis
c. Trend analysis
d. Least squares

8. _____ is a concept that aims to enhance supply chain integration by supporting and assisting joint practices. _____ seeks cooperative management of inventory through joint visibility and replenishment of products throughout the supply chain. Information shared between suppliers and retailers aids in planning and satisfying customer demands through a supportive system of shared information.

a. Groups decision making
b. Timesheets
c. Collaborative Planning, Forecasting and Replenishment
d. Career portfolios

9. A _____ is a form of qualitative research in which a group of people are asked about their attitude towards a product, service, concept, advertisement, idea, or packaging. Questions are asked in an interactive group setting where participants are free to talk with other group members.

The first _____s were created at the Bureau of Applied Social Research by associate director, sociologist Robert K. Merton.

a. Market analysis
b. Focus group
c. Marketing research
d. 1990 Clean Air Act

10. In statistics, many time series exhibit cyclic variation known as _____, periodic variation, or periodic fluctuations. This variation can be either regular or semiregular.

For example, retail sales tend to peak for the Christmas season and then decline after the holidays.

Chapter 12. PLANNING MERCHANDISE ASSORTMENTS

a. 1990 Clean Air Act
b. 28-hour day
c. 33 Strategies of War
d. Seasonality

11. _____ is a recursive process where two or more people or organizations work together in an intersection of common goals -- for example, an intellectual endeavor that is creative in nature--by sharing knowledge, learning and building consensus. _____ does not require leadership and can sometimes bring better results through decentralization and egalitarianism. In particular, teams that work collaboratively can obtain greater resources, recognition and reward when facing competition for finite resources. _____ is also present in opposing goals exhibiting the notion of adversarial _____, though this is not a common case for using the term.

a. 1990 Clean Air Act
b. 28-hour day
c. Collectivism
d. Collaboration

12. _____ is an advertisement in which a particular product specifically mentions a competitor by name for the express purpose of showing why the competitor is inferior to the product naming it.

This should not be confused with parody advertisements, where a fictional product is being advertised for the purpose of poking fun at the particular advertisement, nor should it be confused with the use of a coined brand name for the purpose of comparing the product without actually naming an actual competitor. ('Wikipedia tastes better and is less filling than the Encyclopedia Galactica.')

In the 1980s, during what has been referred to as the cola wars, soft-drink manufacturer Pepsi ran a series of advertisements where people, caught on hidden camera, in a blind taste test, chose Pepsi over rival Coca-Cola.

a. 28-hour day
b. 33 Strategies of War
c. Comparative advertising
d. 1990 Clean Air Act

13. _____ measures the performance of a system. Certain goals are defined and the _____ gives the percentage to which they should be achieved.

Chapter 12. PLANNING MERCHANDISE ASSORTMENTS

Examples

- Percentage of calls answered in a call center.
- Percentage of customers waiting less than a given fixed time.
- Percentage of customers that do not experience a stock out.

_____ is used in supply chain management and in inventory management to measure the performance of inventory systems.

Under stochastic conditions it is unavoidable that in some periods the inventory on hand is not sufficient to deliver the complete demand and, as a consequence, that part of the demand is filled only after an inventory-related waiting time.

a. 33 Strategies of War
b. 1990 Clean Air Act
c. Service level
d. 28-hour day

14. The '_____ scheme' is an economic term, referring to the use of commodity storage for economic stabilization. Specifically, commodities are bought and stored when there is a surplus in the economy and they are sold from these stores when there are shortages in the economy. The institutional buying, storing and selling of commodities by a large player (e.g. a government) can take place for one commodity or a 'basket of commodities'.

a. Reservation wage
b. Buffer stock
c. Contingent employment
d. Power

15. _____ is a term used by inventory specialists to describe a level of extra stock that is maintained below the cycle stock to buffer against stockouts. _____ exists to counter uncertainties in supply and demand. _____ is defined as extra units of inventory carried as protection against possible stockouts .(shortfall in raw material or packaging.)

a. Process automation
b. Product life cycle
c. Knowledge worker
d. Safety stock

16. A _____ is the period of time between the initiation of any process of production and the completion of that process. Thus the _____ for ordering a new car from a manufacturer may be anywhere from 2 weeks to 6 months. In industry, _____ reduction is an important part of lean manufacturing.

a. 28-hour day
b. 1990 Clean Air Act
c. Lead time
d. 33 Strategies of War

Chapter 13. BUYING SYSTEMS

1. _____ is a business term used to define an inventory categorization technique often used in materials management.

   _____ provides a mechanism for identifying items which will have a significant impact on overall inventory cost whilst also providing a mechanism for identifying different categories of stock that will require different management and controls

   When carrying out an _____, inventory items are valued (item cost multiplied by quantity issued/consumed in period) with the results then ranked. The results are then grouped typically into three bands.

   a. A Stake in the Outcome
   b. ABC analysis
   c. AAAI
   d. A4e

2. In economics, _____ is the desire to own something and the ability to pay for it. The term _____ signifies the ability or the willingness to buy a particular commodity at a given point of time.
   a. 28-hour day
   b. 1990 Clean Air Act
   c. 33 Strategies of War
   d. Demand

3. _____ generally refers to a list of all planned expenses and revenues. It is a plan for saving and spending. A _____ is an important concept in microeconomics, which uses a _____ line to illustrate the trade-offs between two or more goods.
   a. 28-hour day
   b. 33 Strategies of War
   c. Budget
   d. 1990 Clean Air Act

4. In cost-volume-profit analysis, a form of management accounting, _____ is the marginal profit per unit sale. It is a useful quantity in carrying out various calculations, and can be used as a measure of operating leverage.

   The Total _____ is Total Revenue (TR, or Sales) minus Total Variable Cost (TVC):

   TContribution margin = TR − TVC

Chapter 13. BUYING SYSTEMS

The Unit _____ (C) is Unit Revenue (Price, P) minus Unit Variable Cost (V):

$$C = P - V$$

The _____ Ratio is the percentage of Contribution over Total Revenue, which can be calculated from the unit contribution over unit price or total contribution over Total Revenue:

$$\frac{C}{P} = \frac{P-V}{P} = \frac{\text{Unit Contribution Margin}}{\text{Price}} = \frac{\text{Total Contribution Margin}}{\text{Total Revenue}}$$

For instance, if the price is $10 and the unit variable cost is $2, then the unit _____ is $8, and the _____ ratio is $8/$10 = 80%.

a. Profit center
b. Factory overhead
c. Contribution margin
d. Customer profitability

5. In economics, business, retail, and accounting, a _____ is the value of money that has been used up to produce something, and hence is not available for use anymore. In economics, a _____ is an alternative that is given up as a result of a decision. In business, the _____ may be one of acquisition, in which case the amount of money expended to acquire it is counted as _____.

a. Cost
b. Cost overrun
c. Cost allocation
d. Fixed costs

6. _____ is the difference between the cost of a good or service and its selling price. A _____ is added on to the total cost incurred by the producer of a good or service in order to create a profit. The total cost reflects the total amount of both fixed and variable expenses to produce and distribute a product.

a. Topics
b. Markup
c. Premium pricing
d. Price points

Chapter 14. BUYING MERCHANDISE

1. A _____ is a name or trademark connected with a product or producer. _____s have become increasingly important components of culture and the economy, now being described as 'cultural accessories and personal philosophies'.

   Some people distinguish the psychological aspect of a _____ from the experiential aspect.

   a. Brand
   b. Brand extension
   c. Brand loyalty
   d. Brand awareness

2. _____ is a term used to describe practice of sourcing from the global market for goods and services across geopolitical boundaries. _____ often aims to exploit global efficiencies in the delivery of a product or service. These efficiencies include low cost skilled labor, low cost raw material and other economic factors like tax breaks and low trade tariffs.
   a. Purchase requisition
   b. Purchasing process
   c. 1990 Clean Air Act
   d. Global sourcing

3. In business, the term word _____ refers to a number of procurement practices, aimed at finding, evaluating and engaging suppliers of goods and services:

   - Global _____, a procurement strategy aimed at exploiting global efficiencies in production
   - Strategic _____, a component of supply chain management, for improving and re-evaluating purchasing activities
   - _____, the identification of job candidates through proactive recruiting technique
   - Co-_____, a type of auditing service
   - Low-cost country _____, a procurement strategy for acquiring materials from countries with lower labour and production costs in order to cut operating expenses
   - Corporate _____, a supply chain, purchasing/procurement, and inventory function
   - Second-tier _____, a practice of rewarding suppliers for attempting to achieve minority-owned business spending goals of their customer
   - Netsourcing, a practice of utilizing an established group of businesses, individuals, or hardware ' software applications to streamline or initiate procurement practices by tapping in to and working through a third party provider
   - Inverted _____, a price volatility reduction strategy usually conducted by procurement or supply-chain person by which the value of an organization's waste-stream is maximized by actively seeking out the highest price possible from a range of potential buyers exploiting price trends and other market factors
   - Multisourcing, a strategy that treats a given function, such as IT, as a portfolio of activities, some of which should be outsourced and others of which should be performed by internal staff.
   - Crowdsourcing, using an undefined, generally large group of people or community in the form of an open call to perform a task

Chapter 14. BUYING MERCHANDISE

In journalism, it can also refer to:

- Journalism _____, the practice of identifying a person or publication that gives information
- Single _____, the reuse of content in publishing

In computing, it can refer to:

- Open-_____, the act of releasing previously proprietary software under an open source/free software license
- Power _____ equipment, network devices that will provide power in a Power over Ethernet (PoE) setup

a. Continuous
b. Reinforcement
c. Sourcing
d. Cost Management

4. _____ is the process of estimation in unknown situations. Prediction is a similar, but more general term. Both can refer to estimation of time series, cross-sectional or longitudinal data.
a. Forecasting
b. 1990 Clean Air Act
c. 33 Strategies of War
d. 28-hour day

5. _____ is a type of trade policy that allows traders to act and transact without interference from government. Thus, the policy permits trading partners mutual gains from trade, with goods and services produced according to the theory of comparative advantage.

Under a _____ policy, prices are a reflection of true supply and demand, and are the sole determinant of resource allocation.

a. 28-hour day
b. 33 Strategies of War
c. 1990 Clean Air Act
d. Free Trade

Chapter 14. BUYING MERCHANDISE

6. _____ is a designated group of countries that have agreed to eliminate tariffs, quotas and preferences on most (if not all) goods and services traded between them. It can be considered the second stage of economic integration. Countries choose this kind of economic integration form if their economical structures are complementary.
    a. 1990 Clean Air Act
    b. Free trade area
    c. 28-hour day
    d. 33 Strategies of War

7. The _____ was the outcome of the failure of negotiating governments to create the International Trade Organization (ITO.) GATT was formed in 1947 and lasted until 1994, when it was replaced by the World Trade Organization. The Bretton Woods Conference had introduced the idea for an organization to regulate trade as part of a larger plan for economic recovery after World War II.
    a. General Agreement on Tariffs and Trade
    b. 28-hour day
    c. Multilateral treaty
    d. 1990 Clean Air Act

8. A _____ or maquila is a factory that imports materials and equipment on a duty-free and tariff-free basis for assembly or manufacturing and then re-exports the assembled product, usually back to the originating country. A maquila is also referred to as a 'twin plant', or 'in-bond' industry. Nearly half a million Mexicans are employed in _____s.
    a. 1990 Clean Air Act
    b. Maquiladora
    c. 28-hour day
    d. 33 Strategies of War

9. The _____ is a trilateral trade bloc in North America created by the governments of the United States, Canada, and Mexico. The agreement creating the trade bloc came into force on January 1, 1994. It superseded the Canada-United States Free Trade Agreement between the U.S. and Canada.
    a. Business war game
    b. Trade union
    c. Career portfolios
    d. North American Free Trade Agreement

Chapter 14. BUYING MERCHANDISE

10. A _____ is a general term that describes any government policy or regulation that restricts international trade. The barriers can take many forms, including the following terms that include many restrictions in international trade within multiple countries that import and export any items of trade.

- Import duty
- Import licenses
- Export licenses
- Import quotas
- Tariffs
- Subsidies
- Non-tariff barriers to trade
- Voluntary Export Restraints
- Local Content Requirements
- Embargo

Most _____s work on the same principle: the imposition of some sort of cost on trade that raises the price of the traded products. If two or more nations repeatedly use _____s against each other, then a trade war results.

a. Trade creation
b. Most favoured nation
c. Customs brokerage
d. Trade barrier

11. A _____ is the period of time between the initiation of any process of production and the completion of that process. Thus the _____ for ordering a new car from a manufacturer may be anywhere from 2 weeks to 6 months. In industry, _____ reduction is an important part of lean manufacturing.

a. 28-hour day
b. 33 Strategies of War
c. 1990 Clean Air Act
d. Lead time

12. _____ or economic opportunity loss is the value of the next best alternative forgone as the result of making a decision. _____ analysis is an important part of a company's decision-making processes but is not treated as an actual cost in any financial statement. The next best thing that a person can engage in is referred to as the _____ of doing the best thing and ignoring the next best thing to be done.

a. A4e
b. A Stake in the Outcome
c. AAAI
d. Opportunity cost

Chapter 14. BUYING MERCHANDISE

13. In economics, business, retail, and accounting, a _____ is the value of money that has been used up to produce something, and hence is not available for use anymore. In economics, a _____ is an alternative that is given up as a result of a decision. In business, the _____ may be one of acquisition, in which case the amount of money expended to acquire it is counted as _____.
    a. Fixed costs
    b. Cost overrun
    c. Cost allocation
    d. Cost

14. The _____ is an expected return that the provider of capital plans to earn on their investment.

    Capital (money) used for funding a business should earn returns for the capital providers who risk their capital. For an investment to be worthwhile, the expected return on capital must be greater than the _____.

    a. 1990 Clean Air Act
    b. Capital intensive
    c. Weighted average cost of capital
    d. Cost of capital

15. _____ is a form of communication that typically attempts to persuade potential customers to purchase or to consume more of a particular brand of product or service. 'While now central to the contemporary global economy and the reproduction of global production networks, it is only quite recently that _____ has been more than a marginal influence on patterns of sales and production. The formation of modern _____ was intimately bound up with the emergence of new forms of monopoly capitalism around the end of the 19th and beginning of the 20th century as one element in corporate strategies to create, organize and where possible control markets, especially for mass produced consumer goods.
    a. A Stake in the Outcome
    b. Advertising
    c. AAAI
    d. A4e

16. The _____ of 1936 (or Anti-Price Discrimination Act, 15 U.S.C. § 13) is a United States federal law that prohibits what were considered, at the time of passage, to be anticompetitive practices by producers, specifically price discrimination. It grew out of practices in which chain stores were allowed to purchase goods at lower prices than other retailers.
    a. Labor Management Reporting and Disclosure Act
    b. Bona fide occupational qualification
    c. Privity
    d. Robinson-Patman Act

Chapter 14. BUYING MERCHANDISE

17. _____ includes dispute resolution processes and techniques that fall outside of the government judicial process. Despite historic resistance to _____ by both parties and their advocates, _____ has gained widespread acceptance among both the general public and the legal profession in recent years. In fact, some courts now require some parties to resort to _____ of some type, usually mediation, before permitting the parties' cases to be tried.
   a. AAAI
   b. Alternative dispute resolution
   c. A Stake in the Outcome
   d. A4e

18. _____, a form of alternative dispute resolution (ADR), is a legal technique for the resolution of disputes outside the courts, wherein the parties to a dispute refer it to one or more persons (the 'arbitrators', 'arbiters' or 'arbitral tribunal'), by whose decision (the 'award') they agree to be bound. It is a settlement technique in which a third party reviews the case and imposes a decision that is legally binding for both sides. Other forms of ADR include mediation (a form of settlement negotiation facilitated by a neutral third party) and non-binding resolution by experts.
   a. Arbitration
   b. A Stake in the Outcome
   c. AAAI
   d. A4e

19. A _____ is the return of funds to a consumer, forcibly initiated by the consumer's issuing bank. Specifically, it is the reversal of a prior outbound transfer of funds from a consumer's bank account or line of credit.

The _____ mechanism exists primarily for consumer protection.

   a. 1990 Clean Air Act
   b. 33 Strategies of War
   c. Chargeback
   d. 28-hour day

20. _____, a form of alternative dispute resolution (ADR) or 'appropriate dispute resolution', aims to assist two (or more) disputants in reaching an agreement. The parties themselves determine the conditions of any settlements reached-- rather than accepting something imposed by a third party. The disputes may involve (as parties) states, organizations, communities, individuals or other representatives with a vested interest in the outcome.
   a. Maximum medical improvement
   b. Foreign Corrupt Practices Act
   c. Meritor Savings Bank v. Vinson
   d. Mediation

Chapter 14. BUYING MERCHANDISE

21. _____ are legal property rights over creations of the mind, both artistic and commercial, and the corresponding fields of law. Under _____ law, owners are granted certain exclusive rights to a variety of intangible assets, such as musical, literary, and artistic works; ideas, discoveries and inventions; and words, phrases, symbols, and designs. Common types of _____ include copyrights, trademarks, patents, industrial design rights and trade secrets.
    a. Unemployment Action Center
    b. Intent
    c. Equal Pay Act
    d. Intellectual property

22. A _____ is a distinctive sign or indicator used by an individual, business organization, or other legal entity to identify that the products and/or services to consumers with which the _____ appears originate from a unique source and to distinguish its products or services from those of other entities.
    a. Kanban
    b. Virtual team
    c. Trademark
    d. Succession planning

23. _____ plant, and equipment, is a term used in accountancy for assets and property which cannot easily be converted into cash. This can be compared with current assets such as cash or bank accounts, which are described as liquid assets. In most cases, only tangible assets are referred to as fixed.
    a. 33 Strategies of War
    b. 28-hour day
    c. 1990 Clean Air Act
    d. Fixed asset

24. A _____ is an alliance among individuals or groups, during which they cooperate in joint action, each in his own self-interest, joining forces together for a common cause. This alliance may be temporary or a matter of convenience. A _____ thus differs from a more formal covenant.
    a. 28-hour day
    b. 1990 Clean Air Act
    c. 33 Strategies of War
    d. Coalition

Chapter 15. PRICING

1. _____ is one of the four Ps of the marketing mix. The other three aspects are product, promotion, and place. It is also a key variable in microeconomic price allocation theory.

    a. Price floor
    b. Penetration pricing
    c. Transfer pricing
    d. Pricing

2. The act of becoming a surety is also called a _____. Traditionally a _____ was distinguished from a surety in that the surety's liability was joint and primary with the principal, whereas the guaranty's liability was ancillary and derivative, but many jurisdictions have abolished this distinction

    a. Clayton Antitrust Act
    b. Blue sky law
    c. National treatment
    d. Guarantee

3. A _____ is typically described as a deliberate plan of action to guide decisions and achieve rational outcome(s.) However, the term may also be used to denote what is actually done, even though it is unplanned.

    The term may apply to government, private sector organizations and groups, and individuals.

    a. Policy
    b. 33 Strategies of War
    c. 1990 Clean Air Act
    d. 28-hour day

4. _____ is an advertisement in which a particular product specifically mentions a competitor by name for the express purpose of showing why the competitor is inferior to the product naming it.

    This should not be confused with parody advertisements, where a fictional product is being advertised for the purpose of poking fun at the particular advertisement, nor should it be confused with the use of a coined brand name for the purpose of comparing the product without actually naming an actual competitor. ('Wikipedia tastes better and is less filling than the Encyclopedia Galactica.')

    In the 1980s, during what has been referred to as the cola wars, soft-drink manufacturer Pepsi ran a series of advertisements where people, caught on hidden camera, in a blind taste test, chose Pepsi over rival Coca-Cola.

Chapter 15. PRICING

a. 33 Strategies of War
b. 28-hour day
c. Comparative advertising
d. 1990 Clean Air Act

5. _____ is the difference between the cost of a good or service and its selling price. A _____ is added on to the total cost incurred by the producer of a good or service in order to create a profit. The total cost reflects the total amount of both fixed and variable expenses to produce and distribute a product.

a. Premium pricing
b. Price points
c. Topics
d. Markup

6. In economics ' business, specifically cost accounting, the _____ is the point at which cost or expenses and revenue are equal: there is no net loss or gain, and one has 'broken even'. A profit or a loss has not been made, although opportunity costs have been paid, and capital has received the risk-adjusted, expected return.

For example, if the business sells less than 200 tables each month, it will make a loss, if it sells more, it will be a profit.

a. Fixed asset turnover
b. Virtuous circle
c. Defined benefit pension plan
d. Break-even point

7. In economics, _____ are business expenses that are not dependent on the activities of the business They tend to be time-related, such as salaries or rents being paid per month. This is in contrast to variable costs, which are volume-related (and are paid per quantity.)

In management accounting, _____ are defined as expenses that do not change in proportion to the activity of a business, within the relevant period or scale of production.

a. Transaction cost
b. Cost allocation
c. Cost of quality
d. Fixed costs

Chapter 15. PRICING

8. _____s are expenses that change in proportion to the activity of a business. In other words, _____ is the sum of marginal costs. It can also be considered normal costs.
   a. Cost accounting
   b. Fixed costs
   c. Cost overrun
   d. Variable cost

9. In economics, business, retail, and accounting, a _____ is the value of money that has been used up to produce something, and hence is not available for use anymore. In economics, a _____ is an alternative that is given up as a result of a decision. In business, the _____ may be one of acquisition, in which case the amount of money expended to acquire it is counted as _____.
   a. Cost allocation
   b. Cost
   c. Cost overrun
   d. Fixed costs

10. In cost-volume-profit analysis, a form of management accounting, _____ is the marginal profit per unit sale. It is a useful quantity in carrying out various calculations, and can be used as a measure of operating leverage.

The Total _____ is Total Revenue (TR, or Sales) minus Total Variable Cost (TVC):

TContribution margin = TR − TVC

The Unit _____ (C) is Unit Revenue (Price, P) minus Unit Variable Cost (V):

C = P − V

The _____ Ratio is the percentage of Contribution over Total Revenue, which can be calculated from the unit contribution over unit price or total contribution over Total Revenue:

$$\frac{C}{P} = \frac{P-V}{P} = \frac{\text{Unit Contribution Margin}}{\text{Price}} = \frac{\text{Total Contribution Margin}}{\text{Total Revenue}}$$

For instance, if the price is $10 and the unit variable cost is $2, then the unit _____ is $8, and the _____ ratio is $8/$10 = 80%.

a. Customer profitability
b. Contribution margin
c. Factory overhead
d. Profit center

11. _____ is a lightweight markup language, originally created by John Gruber and Aaron Swartz to help maximum readability and 'publishability' of both its input and output forms. The language takes many cues from existing conventions for marking up plain text in email. _____ converts its marked-up text input to valid, well-formed XHTML and replaces left-pointing angle brackets ('<') and ampersands with their corresponding character entity references.

a. 33 Strategies of War
b. 28-hour day
c. 1990 Clean Air Act
d. Markdown

12. The _____ of 1936 (or Anti-Price Discrimination Act, 15 U.S.C. § 13) is a United States federal law that prohibits what were considered, at the time of passage, to be anticompetitive practices by producers, specifically price discrimination. It grew out of practices in which chain stores were allowed to purchase goods at lower prices than other retailers.

a. Bona fide occupational qualification
b. Labor Management Reporting and Disclosure Act
c. Privity
d. Robinson-Patman Act

13. _____ exists when sales of identical goods or services are transacted at different prices from the same provider. In a theoretical market with perfect information, no transaction costs or prohibition on secondary exchange (or re-selling) to prevent arbitrage, _____ can only be a feature of monopoly and oligopoly markets, where market power can be exercised. Otherwise, the moment the seller tries to sell the same good at different prices, the buyer at the lower price can arbitrage by selling to the consumer buying at the higher price but with a tiny discount.

a. Pricing objectives
b. Price discrimination
c. Price points
d. Target costing

14. _____ is a form of communication that typically attempts to persuade potential customers to purchase or to consume more of a particular brand of product or service. 'While now central to the contemporary global economy and the reproduction of global production networks, it is only quite recently that _____ has been more than a marginal influence on patterns of sales and production. The formation of modern _____ was intimately bound up with the emergence of new forms of monopoly capitalism around the end of the 19th and beginning of the 20th century as one element in corporate strategies to create, organize and where possible control markets, especially for mass produced consumer goods.

Chapter 15. PRICING

a. A Stake in the Outcome
b. Advertising
c. AAAI
d. A4e

15. In marketing a _____ is a ticket or document that can be exchanged for a financial discount or rebate when purchasing a product. Customarily, _____s are issued by manufacturers of consumer packaged goods or by retailers, to be used in retail stores as a part of sales promotions. They are often widely distributed through mail, magazines, newspapers, the Internet, and mobile devices such as cell phones.

a. Word of mouth
b. Sales promotion
c. 1990 Clean Air Act
d. Coupon

16. _____, commonly known as e-commerce, consists of the buying and selling of products or services over electronic systems such as the Internet and other computer networks. The amount of trade conducted electronically has grown extraordinarily with widespread Internet usage. The use of commerce is conducted in this way, spurring and drawing on innovations in electronic funds transfer, supply chain management, Internet marketing, online transaction processing, electronic data interchange (EDI), inventory management systems, and automated data collection systems.

a. A Stake in the Outcome
b. A4e
c. Online shopping
d. Electronic Commerce

17. _____ is the practice of selling a product or service at a very low price, intending to drive competitors out of the market, or create barriers to entry for potential new competitors. If competitors or potential competitors cannot sustain equal or lower prices without losing money, they go out of business or choose not to enter the business. The predatory merchant then has fewer competitors or is even a de facto monopoly, and can then raise prices above what the market would otherwise bear.

a. Collusion
b. 28-hour day
c. 1990 Clean Air Act
d. Predatory pricing

18. _____ is a broad label that refers to any individuals or households that use goods and services generated within the economy. The concept of a _____ is used in different contexts, so that the usage and significance of the term may vary.

Chapter 15. PRICING

Typically when business people and economists talk of _____s they are talking about person as _____, an aggregated commodity item with little individuality other than that expressed in the buy/not-buy decision.

a. Consumer
b. 1990 Clean Air Act
c. 33 Strategies of War
d. 28-hour day

19. _____ is an organized social movement and market-based approach that aims to help producers in developing countries and promote sustainability. The movement advocates the payment of a higher price to producers as well as social and environmental standards in areas related to the production of a wide variety of goods. It focuses in particular on exports from developing countries to developed countries, most notably handicrafts, coffee, cocoa, sugar, tea, bananas, honey, cotton, wine, fresh fruit, chocolate and flowers.

a. 1990 Clean Air Act
b. 33 Strategies of War
c. 28-hour day
d. Fair trade

20. Price fixing is an agreement between business competitors to sell the same product or service at the same price. In general, it is an agreement intended to ultimately push the price of a product as high as possible, leading to profits for all the sellers. _____ can also involve any agreement to fix, peg, discount or stabilize prices.

a. 33 Strategies of War
b. 28-hour day
c. 1990 Clean Air Act
d. Price-fixing

21. In retail sales, a _____ is a form of fraud in which the party putting forth the fraud lures in customers by advertising a product or service at an unprofitably low price, then reveals to potential customers that the advertised good is not available but that a substitute is. This term has lots of other meanings, even outside of the marketing sense.

The goal of the _____ is to convince some buyers to purchase the substitute good as a means of avoiding disappointment over not getting the bait, or as a way to recover sunk costs expended to try to obtain the bait.

a. 28-hour day
b. 33 Strategies of War
c. 1990 Clean Air Act
d. Bait and switch

22. In the fields of science, engineering, industry and statistics, _____ is the degree of closeness of a measured or calculated quantity to its actual (true) value. _____ is closely related to precision, also called reproducibility or repeatability, the degree to which further measurements or calculations show the same or similar results. _____ indicates proximity to the true value, precision to the repeatability or reproducibility of the measurement

The results of calculations or a measurement can be accurate but not precise, precise but not accurate, neither, or both.

a. A4e
b. AAAI
c. Accuracy
d. A Stake in the Outcome

23. The general definition of an _____ is an evaluation of a person, organization, system, process, project or product. _____s are performed to ascertain the validity and reliability of information; also to provide an assessment of a system's internal control. The goal of an _____ is to express an opinion on the person / organization/system (etc) in question, under evaluation based on work done on a test basis.
a. Audit committee
b. Audit
c. A Stake in the Outcome
d. Internal control

Chapter 16. RETAIL COMMUNICATION MIX 75

1. A _____ is a name or trademark connected with a product or producer. _____s have become increasingly important components of culture and the economy, now being described as 'cultural accessories and personal philosophies'.

Some people distinguish the psychological aspect of a _____ from the experiential aspect.

a. Brand loyalty
b. Brand
c. Brand awareness
d. Brand extension

2. _____ is a marketing concept that refers to a consumer knowing of a brand's existence; at aggregate (brand) level it refers to the proportion of consumers who know of the brand.

_____ can be measured by showing a consumer the brand and asking whether or not they knew of it beforehand. However, in common market research practice a variety of recognition and recall measures of _____ are employed all of which test the brand name's association to a product category cue, this came about because most market research in the 20th Century was conducted by post or telephone, actually showing the brand to consumers usually required more expensive face-to-face interviews (until web-based interviews became possible.)

a. Channel conflict
b. Brand management
c. Brand loyalty
d. Brand awareness

3. Some people distinguish the psychological aspect of a brand from the experiential aspect. The experiential aspect consists of the sum of all points of contact with the brand and is known as the brand experience. The psychological aspect, sometimes referred to as the _____, is a symbolic construct created within the minds of people and consists of all the information and expectations associated with a product or service.
a. Channel conflict
b. Brand awareness
c. Brand management
d. Brand image

4. _____ is an integrated communications-based process through which individuals and communities discover that existing and newly-identified needs and wants may be satisfied by the products and services of others.

Chapter 16. RETAIL COMMUNICATION MIX

_____ is defined by the American _____ Association as the activity, set of institutions, and processes for creating, communicating, delivering, and exchanging offerings that have value for customers, clients, partners, and society at large. The term developed from the original meaning which referred literally to going to market, as in shopping, or going to a market to buy or sell goods or services.

a. Disruptive technology
b. Customer relationship management
c. Market development
d. Marketing

5. _____s (or MarCom or Integrated _____s) are messages and related media used to communicate with a market. Those who practice advertising, branding, direct marketing, graphic design, marketing, packaging, promotion, publicity, sponsorship, public relations, sales, sales promotion and online marketing are termed marketing communicators, _____ managers, or more briefly as marcom managers.

Traditionally, _____ practitioners focus on the creation and execution of printed marketing collateral; however, academic and professional research developed the practice to use strategic elements of branding and marketing in order to ensure consistency of message delivery throughout an organization.

a. Thomas Dale DeLay
b. Abraham Harold Maslow
c. Adam Smith
d. Marketing communication

6. _____ is a form of communication that typically attempts to persuade potential customers to purchase or to consume more of a particular brand of product or service. 'While now central to the contemporary global economy and the reproduction of global production networks, it is only quite recently that _____ has been more than a marginal influence on patterns of sales and production. The formation of modern _____ was intimately bound up with the emergence of new forms of monopoly capitalism around the end of the 19th and beginning of the 20th century as one element in corporate strategies to create, organize and where possible control markets, especially for mass produced consumer goods.

a. A4e
b. AAAI
c. A Stake in the Outcome
d. Advertising

7. An _____ is a series of advertisement messages that share a single idea and theme which make up an integrated marketing communication (IMC.) _____s appear in different media across a specific time frame.

Chapter 16. RETAIL COMMUNICATION MIX 77

The critical part of making an _____ is determining a champion theme, as it sets the tone for the individual advertisements and other forms of marketing communications that will be used.

a. A4e
b. AAAI
c. A Stake in the Outcome
d. Advertising campaign

8. _____ generally refers to a list of all planned expenses and revenues. It is a plan for saving and spending. A _____ is an important concept in microeconomics, which uses a _____ line to illustrate the trade-offs between two or more goods.
a. 33 Strategies of War
b. 28-hour day
c. Budget
d. 1990 Clean Air Act

9. In marketing a _____ is a ticket or document that can be exchanged for a financial discount or rebate when purchasing a product. Customarily, _____s are issued by manufacturers of consumer packaged goods or by retailers, to be used in retail stores as a part of sales promotions. They are often widely distributed through mail, magazines, newspapers, the Internet, and mobile devices such as cell phones.
a. Word of mouth
b. Coupon
c. 1990 Clean Air Act
d. Sales promotion

10. _____ is one of the four aspects of promotional mix. (The other three parts of the promotional mix are advertising, personal selling, and publicity/public relations.) Media and non-media marketing communication are employed for a pre-determined, limited time to increase consumer demand, stimulate market demand or improve product availability.
a. Coupon
b. 1990 Clean Air Act
c. Word of mouth
d. Sales promotion

11. _____ consists of the sale of goods or merchandise from a fixed location, such as a department store, boutique or kiosk in small or individual lots for direct consumption by the purchaser. _____ may include subordinated services, such as delivery. Purchasers may be individuals or businesses.

Chapter 16. RETAIL COMMUNICATION MIX

a. Planogram
b. 1990 Clean Air Act
c. 28-hour day
d. Retailing

12. _____ is a reference to the passing of information from person to person. Originally the term referred specifically to oral communication (literally words from the mouth), but now includes any type of human communication, such as face to face, telephone, email, and text messaging.

One of the earliest Australasian references to and the active use of the term '_____ Marketing' was by an Australian MLM company from the mid 1980's.

a. Sales promotion
b. Word of mouth
c. Coupon
d. 1990 Clean Air Act

13. _____ systems are rule-based systems that are able to automatically provide solutions to repetitive management problems (Turban, Leidner, McLean and Wetherbe, 2007.) _____s are very closely related to business informatics and business analytics.

_____ systems are based on business rules.

a. Efficient Consumer Response
b. Executive development
c. Entertainment Management
d. Automated decision support

14. In economics, business, retail, and accounting, a _____ is the value of money that has been used up to produce something, and hence is not available for use anymore. In economics, a _____ is an alternative that is given up as a result of a decision. In business, the _____ may be one of acquisition, in which case the amount of money expended to acquire it is counted as _____.

a. Cost allocation
b. Fixed costs
c. Cost
d. Cost overrun

Chapter 17. MANAGING THE STORE

1. _____ refers to various methodologies for analyzing the requirements of a job.

The general purpose of _____ is to document the requirements of a job and the work performed. Job and task analysis is performed as a basis for later improvements, including: definition of a job domain; describing a job; developing performance appraisals, selection systems, promotion criteria, training needs assessment, and compensation plans.

   a. Management process
   b. Job analysis
   c. Hersey-Blanchard situational theory
   d. Work design

2. A _____ is a list of the general tasks and responsibilities of a position. Typically, it also includes to whom the position reports, specifications such as the qualifications needed by the person in the job, salary range for the position, etc. A _____ is usually developed by conducting a job analysis, which includes examining the tasks and sequences of tasks necessary to perform the job.
   a. Recruitment Process Insourcing
   b. Recruitment advertising
   c. Recruitment
   d. Job description

3. A _____ is a process in which a potential employee is evaluated by an employer for prospective employment in their company, organization and was established in the late 16th century.

A _____ typically precedes the hiring decision, and is used to evaluate the candidate. The interview is usually preceded by the evaluation of submitted résumés from interested candidates, then selecting a small number of candidates for interviews.

   a. Supported employment
   b. Split shift
   c. Payrolling
   d. Job interview

4. In US employment law, _____ is defined as a substantially different rate of selection in hiring, promotion sex statistical significance tests, and/or practical significance tests. _____ is often used interchangeably with 'disparate impact,' which was a legal term coined in one of the most significant U.S. Supreme Court rulings on disparate or _____: Griggs v. Duke Power Co., 1971.

Chapter 17. MANAGING THE STORE

a. AAAI
b. A Stake in the Outcome
c. A4e
d. Adverse impact

5. _____ is a contract between two parties, one being the employer and the other being the employee. An employee may be defined as: 'A person in the service of another under any contract of hire, express or implied, oral or written, where the employer has the power or right to control and direct the employee in the material details of how the work is to be performed.' Black's Law Dictionary page 471 (5th ed. 1979.)
   a. Employment
   b. Employment counsellor
   c. Exit interview
   d. Employment rate

6. The term _____ was created by President Lyndon B. Johnson when he signed Executive Order 11246 on September 24, 1965, created to prohibit federal contractors from discriminating against employees on the basis of race, sex, creed, religion, color, or national origin. In more recent times, most employers have also added sexual orientation to the list of non-discrimination.

The Executive Order also required contractors to implement affirmative action plans to increase the participation of minorities and women in the workplace.

   a. AAAI
   b. A4e
   c. A Stake in the Outcome
   d. Equal Employment Opportunity

7. The U.S. _____ is a federal agency whose goal is ending employment discrimination. The _____ investigates discrimination complaints based on an individual's race, color, national origin, religion, sex, age, disability and retaliation for reporting and/or opposing a discriminatory practice. The Commission is also tasked with filing suits on behalf of alleged victim(s) of discrimination against employers and as an adjudicatory for claims of discrimination brought against federal agencies.
   a. Airbus SAS
   b. ARCO
   c. Airbus Industrie
   d. Equal Employment Opportunity Commission

Chapter 17. MANAGING THE STORE 81

8. A _____ is one scenario provided for evaluation by respondents in a Choice Experiment. Responses are collected and used to create a Choice Model. Respondents are usually provided with a series of differing _____s for evaluation.
   a. Pairwise comparison
   b. Computerized classification test
   c. Thurstone scale
   d. Choice Set

9. _____ has been described as the 'process of social influence in which one person can enlist the aid and support of others in the accomplishment of a common task' . A definition more inclusive of followers comes from Alan Keith of Genentech who said '_____ is ultimately about creating a way for people to contribute to making something extraordinary happen.'

_____ is one of the most salient aspects of the organizational context. However, defining _____ has been challenging.

   a. 28-hour day
   b. Leadership
   c. 1990 Clean Air Act
   d. Situational leadership

10. _____ is unwelcome harassment of a sexual nature, or based upon the receiving party's sex or gender. In some contexts or circumstances, _____ may be illegal. It includes a range of behavior from seemingly mild transgressions and annoyances to actual sexual abuse or sexual assault.
    a. Sexual harassment
    b. 28-hour day
    c. Hypernorms
    d. 1990 Clean Air Act

11. In economics and sociology, an _____ is any factor (financial or non-financial) that enables or motivates a particular course of action, or counts as a reason for preferring one choice to the alternatives. It is an expectation that encourages people to behave in a certain way. Since human beings are purposeful creatures, the study of _____ structures is central to the study of all economic activity (both in terms of individual decision-making and in terms of co-operation and competition within a larger institutional structure.)
    a. Incentive
    b. A4e
    c. AAAI
    d. A Stake in the Outcome

Chapter 17. MANAGING THE STORE

12. _____ is an attempt to motivate employees by giving them the opportunity to use the range of their abilities. It is an idea that was developed by the American psychologist Frederick Herzberg in the 1950s. It can be contrasted to job enlargement which simply increases the number of tasks without changing the challenge.
   a. C-A-K-E
   b. Job enrichment
   c. Cash cow
   d. Catfish effect

13. The _____ 1970 is an Act of the United Kingdom Parliament which prohibits any less favourable treatment between men and women in terms of pay and conditions of employment. It came into force on 29 December 1975. The term pay is interpreted in a broad sense to include, on top of wages, things like holidays, pension rights, company perks and some kinds of bonuses.
   a. Australian labour law
   b. Oncale v. Sundowner Offshore Services
   c. Equal Pay Act
   d. Architectural Barriers Act of 1968

14. The _____ of 1938 (_____, ch. 676, 52 Stat. 1060, June 25, 1938, 29 U.S.C. ch.8), also called the Wages and Hours Bill, is United States federal law that applies to employees engaged in interstate commerce or employed by an enterprise engaged in commerce or in the production of goods for commerce, unless the employer can claim an exemption from coverage. The _____ established a national minimum wage, guaranteed time and a half for overtime in certain jobs, and prohibited most employment of minors in 'oppressive child labor,' a term defined in the statute.
   a. Family and Medical Leave Act of 1993
   b. Joint venture
   c. Fair Labor Standards Act
   d. Board of directors

15. _____ are conventions, treaties and recommendations designed to eliminate unjust and inhumane labour practices. The primary inernational agency charged with developing such standards is the International Labour Organization (ILO.) Established in 1919, the ILO advocates international standards as essential for the eradication of labour conditions involving 'injustice, hardship and privation'.
   a. Anaconda Copper
   b. Airbus Industrie
   c. Airbus SAS
   d. International labour standards

16. The _____ captures an expanded spectrum of values and criteria for measuring organizational success: economic, ecological and social. With the ratification of the United Nations and ICLEI _____ standard for urban and community accounting in early 2007, this became the dominant approach to public sector full cost accounting. Similar UN standards apply to natural capital and human capital measurement to assist in measurements required by _____, e.g. the ecoBudget standard for reporting ecological footprint.

   a. 28-hour day
   b. 33 Strategies of War
   c. 1990 Clean Air Act
   d. Triple bottom line

Chapter 18. STORE LAYOUT, DESIGN, AND VISUAL MERCHANDISING

1. A _____ is a diagram of fixtures and products that illustrates how and where retail products should be displayed, usually on a store shelf in order to increase customer purchases. They may also be referred to as plano-grams, plan-o-grams, schematics (archaic) or POGs.

A _____ is often received before a product reaches a store, and is useful when a retailer wants multiple store displays to have the same look and feel.

a. 1990 Clean Air Act
b. 28-hour day
c. Retailing
d. Planogram

Chapter 19. CUSTOMER SERVICE

1. _____ is the provision of service to customers before, during and after a purchase.

According to Turban et al. (2002), '_____ is a series of activities designed to enhance the level of customer satisfaction - that is, the feeling that a product or service has met the customer expectation.'

Its importance varies by product, industry and customer; defective or broken merchandise can be exchanged, often only with a receipt and within a specified time frame.

   a. Service rate
   b. 28-hour day
   c. 1990 Clean Air Act
   d. Customer service

2. _____ is an advertisement in which a particular product specifically mentions a competitor by name for the express purpose of showing why the competitor is inferior to the product naming it.

This should not be confused with parody advertisements, where a fictional product is being advertised for the purpose of poking fun at the particular advertisement, nor should it be confused with the use of a coined brand name for the purpose of comparing the product without actually naming an actual competitor. ('Wikipedia tastes better and is less filling than the Encyclopedia Galactica.')

In the 1980s, during what has been referred to as the cola wars, soft-drink manufacturer Pepsi ran a series of advertisements where people, caught on hidden camera, in a blind taste test, chose Pepsi over rival Coca-Cola.

   a. 28-hour day
   b. 33 Strategies of War
   c. 1990 Clean Air Act
   d. Comparative advertising

3. _____ is a term defined by the Oxford English Dictionary as an individual's 'course or progress through life '. It is usually considered to pertain to remunerative work (and sometimes also formal education.)

The etymology of the term is somewhat ironic in that it comes from the Latin word carrera, which means race .

   a. Spatial mismatch
   b. Career
   c. Career planning
   d. Nursing shortage

Chapter 19. CUSTOMER SERVICE

4. In economics, business, retail, and accounting, a _____ is the value of money that has been used up to produce something, and hence is not available for use anymore. In economics, a _____ is an alternative that is given up as a result of a decision. In business, the _____ may be one of acquisition, in which case the amount of money expended to acquire it is counted as _____.

   a. Cost allocation
   b. Cost overrun
   c. Fixed costs
   d. Cost

5. Mystery shopping or Mystery Consumer is a tool used by market research companies to measure quality of retail service or gather specific information about products and services. _____ posing as normal customers perform specific tasks-- such as purchasing a product, asking questions, registering complaints or behaving in a certain way - and then provide detailed reports or feedback about their experiences.

   Mystery shopping began in the 1940s as a way to measure employee integrity.

   a. Mystery shoppers
   b. Questionnaire
   c. Quantitative marketing research
   d. Questionnaire construction

6. _____ refers to increasing the spiritual, political, social or economic strength of individuals and communities. It often involves the empowered developing confidence in their own capacities.

   The term Human _____ covers a vast landscape of meanings, interpretations, definitions and disciplines ranging from psychology and philosophy to the highly commercialized Self-Help industry and Motivational sciences.

   a. AAAI
   b. A4e
   c. A Stake in the Outcome
   d. Empowerment

ANSWER KEY

Chapter 1
    1. d   2. c   3. c   4. b   5. a   6. a   7. b

Chapter 2
    1. b   2. a   3. d   4. c   5. b   6. d   7. a   8. d   9. d   10. d
    11. d   12. d   13. d   14. b   15. d   16. a   17. d   18. a

Chapter 3
    1. c   2. d   3. a   4. d   5. b   6. d   7. b   8. d   9. d

Chapter 4
    1. d   2. d   3. b   4. d   5. c   6. c   7. d   8. a   9. d   10. b
    11. c

Chapter 5
    1. c   2. c   3. a   4. d   5. d   6. c   7. d   8. d   9. a   10. c
    11. d   12. d   13. d   14. d   15. b   16. c   17. d   18. b   19. a   20. d
    21. c   22. b   23. d   24. c   25. d   26. d   27. d

Chapter 6
    1. d   2. d   3. b   4. d   5. d   6. d   7. d   8. d   9. a   10. d
    11. d   12. c   13. b   14. a   15. b   16. a   17. c   18. a   19. b   20. d
    21. d

Chapter 7
    1. a   2. d   3. a

Chapter 8
    1. b   2. d   3. d   4. d   5. b   6. d   7. c   8. d   9. c   10. a
    11. c   12. d   13. d

Chapter 9
    1. d   2. a   3. d   4. b   5. b   6. d   7. c   8. d   9. a   10. a
    11. c   12. b   13. c   14. c   15. b   16. d   17. c   18. d   19. a   20. b
    21. d   22. d   23. c   24. d   25. d   26. a

Chapter 10
    1. b   2. a   3. b   4. b   5. c   6. c   7. a   8. d   9. d   10. c
    11. c   12. d   13. d   14. b   15. b   16. b   17. c   18. a   19. a   20. d
    21. d

Chapter 11
    1. d   2. a   3. d   4. d   5. d   6. a   7. d   8. b   9. d   10. b
    11. d   12. d   13. c

Chapter 12
1. c   2. d   3. d   4. b   5. d   6. b   7. c   8. c   9. b   10. d
11. d   12. c   13. c   14. b   15. d   16. c

Chapter 13
1. b   2. d   3. c   4. c   5. a   6. b

Chapter 14
1. a   2. d   3. c   4. a   5. d   6. b   7. a   8. b   9. d   10. d
11. d   12. d   13. d   14. d   15. b   16. d   17. b   18. a   19. c   20. d
21. d   22. c   23. d   24. d

Chapter 15
1. d   2. d   3. a   4. c   5. d   6. d   7. d   8. d   9. b   10. b
11. d   12. d   13. b   14. b   15. d   16. d   17. d   18. a   19. d   20. d
21. d   22. c   23. b

Chapter 16
1. b   2. d   3. d   4. d   5. d   6. d   7. d   8. c   9. b   10. d
11. d   12. b   13. d   14. c

Chapter 17
1. b   2. d   3. d   4. d   5. a   6. d   7. d   8. d   9. b   10. a
11. a   12. b   13. c   14. c   15. d   16. d

Chapter 18
1. d

Chapter 19
1. d   2. d   3. b   4. d   5. a   6. d

www.ingramcontent.com/pod-product-compliance
Lightning Source LLC
Chambersburg PA
CBHW081848230426
43669CB00018B/2863